FINGERSTYLE FOR NOOBS

How to decode & progress with fingerstyle guitar in under 23 days

140 exercises included

GUITAR HEAD

GH@theguitarhead.com
facebook.com/theguitarhead
instagram.com/theguitarhead

©Copyright 2022 by Guitar Head - All rights reserved.

This document is geared towards providing exact and reliable information in regard to the topic and issue covered. The publication is sold with the idea that the publisher is not required to render accounting, officially permitted, or otherwise, qualified services. If advice is necessary, legal or professional, a practiced individual in the profession should be ordered.

- From a Declaration of Principles which was accepted and approved equally by a Committee of the American Bar Association and a Committee of Publishers and Associations.

In no way is it legal to reproduce, duplicate, or transmit any part of this document in either electronic means or in printed format. Recording of this publication is strictly prohibited and any storage of this document is not allowed unless with written permission from the publisher. All rights reserved.

The information provided herein is stated to be truthful and consistent, in that any liability, in terms of inattention or otherwise, by any usage or abuse of any policies, processes, or directions contained within is the solitary and utter responsibility of the recipient reader. Under no circumstances will any legal responsibility or blame be held against the publisher for any reparation, damages, or monetary loss due to the information herein, either directly or indirectly.

Respective authors own all copyrights not held by the publisher.

The information herein is offered for informational purposes solely and is universal as so. The presentation of the information is without contract or any type of guaranteed assurance.

The trademarks that are used are without any consent, and the publication of the trademark is without permission or backing by the trademark owner. All trademarks and brands within this book are for clarifying purposes only and are the owned by the owners themselves, not affiliated with this document.

Disclaimer

Please note the information contained within this document is for educational and entertainment purposes only. Every attempt has been made to provide accurate, up to date and reliable complete information. No warranties of any kind are expressed or implied. Readers acknowledge that the author is not engaging in the rendering of legal and financial, medical or professional advice. The content of this book has been derived from various sources. Please consult a licensed professional before attempting any techniques outline in this book.
By reading this document, the reader agrees that under no circumstances are is the author responsible for any losses, direct or indirect, which are incurred as a result of the use of information contained within this document, including, but not limited to, - errors, omissions, or inaccuracies.

Dedication

*We dedicate this book to the complete
Guitar Head team,
supporters, well-wishers and
the Guitar Head community.*

*It goes without saying that we
would not have gotten
this far without
your encouragement,
critique and support*

Table of Contents

Free Guitar Head Bonuses 8

Book Profile 10

Introduction 11
   Who is this book for? 11
   Why learn fingerstyle guitar? 12

Guitar Tablature What It Is and How to Use It 14

PART 1: FIRST 23 DAYS 17

Level 1 : Getting Started 19
   The pima notation 19
   The rule of thumb 20
   Right hand position 21
   Thumb exercises 23
   Practicing with a metronome 25
   Few more exercises 26
   Commonly asked questions 30
   Conclusion 32

Level 2 : Finger Team Work 33
   Conclusion 41

Level 3 : Arpeggios 43
   Patterns 43
   Conclusion 52

Level 4 : Getting Ready For The Real World 53

Conclusion 63

Level 5 : You're A Bass Player Now 65
Walking bass 71
Conclusion 78

Level 6 : Arranging Simple Songs 79
Happy Birthday 79
Oh When the Saints Go Marching In 81
Conclusion 83

Level 7 : Essential Techniques 85
Hammer-on 85
Pull-off 87
Harmonics 88
Slapping thumb 91
Conclusion 93

PART 2: KEEP YOUR JOURNEY GOING 17

Chapter 1 : Licks In The Style Of Greats 97
Travis Picking 97
James Taylor 100
Simon & Garfunkel 101
Chet Atkins 102
Tommy Emmanuel 104
Mauro Giuliani 105
Conclusion 110

Chapter 2 : More Pieces 113
Camp Town Races 114
Auld Lang Syne 117
Amazing Grace 119
Conclusion 123

Farewell 125

Free Guitar Head Bonuses

Audio Files

All Guitar Head books come with audio tracks for the licks inside the book. These audio tracks are an integral part of the book - they ensure you are playing the charts and chords the way they are intended to be played.

Lifetime access to Guitar Head Community

Being around like-minded people is the first step to being successful at anything. The Guitar Head community is a place where you can find people who are willing to listen to your music, answer your questions or talk anything guitar.

Email Newsletters Sent Directly to Your Inbox

We send regular guitar lessons and tips to all our subscribers. Our subscribers are also the first to know about Guitar Head giveaways and holiday discounts.

Free PDF

Guitar mastery is all about the details! Getting the small things right and avoiding mistakes that can slow your guitar journey by years. So, we wrote a book about 25 of the most common mistakes guitarists make and decided to give it for free to all Guitar Head readers.

You can grab a copy of the free book, the audio files and subscribe to the newsletter by following the link below.

All these bonuses are a 100% free, with no strings attached. You won't need to enter any personal details other than your first name and email address.

To get your bonuses, go to: *www.theguitarhead.com/bonus*

Book Profile

Difficulty Level: Beginner - Intermediate

Technical knowledge you need before reading this book:

Fingerstyle For Noobs - covers everything you need as a beginner to step into the world of fingerstyle guitar. However, to stay true to the concept of fingerstyle, I will not be discussing the basics of guitar playing.

So I recommend the following skills before getting into this book:

- Basics of guitar - tuning, how to hold, basic finger independence etc.
- Knowledge of open chords.
- Basics of rhythm.
- Knowledge of chord progressions.

Suggested reading before this book:

If you are in the "just got a guitar" phase, you can check out our *Guitar Exercises for Beginner* book which will teach you the fundamentals before getting into fingerstyle.

Introduction

Who is this book for?

Welcome to Fingerstyle Guitar for Noobs!

This book is for beginner to intermediate players who are interested in learning the basics of fingerstyle guitar. It doesn't matter if you only know a few chords on the acoustic guitar or if you're a solo shredding machine on your electric guitar. If you are just starting to play with your right hand fingers, this book is for you.

I will guide you through your first steps in learning how to play fingerpicking guitar, teaching you the basic and not-so-basic techniques. We'll go through theory, practical exercises, and a few fingerpicking songs to consolidate your learnings.

In the first part of this book, we'll cover everything you need to start your journey with fingerstyle guitar. Our goal is to finish the first section in 23 days, so you have the basics under your belt as soon as possible.

Each level of the first part of this book comes with a recommended timeline which will total to 23 days. The second part of the book is some "keep progressing" material which you can take your own time with. It also includes exercises you can practice on a daily basis, licks in the style of famous guitarists and a few advanced arrangements of songs.

By the end of the book, you'll have the tools you'll need to play fingerpicking guitar, and by then the only thing that will separate you from becoming an advanced player will be the amount of practice and dedication you'll put in.

Why learn fingerstyle guitar?

Learning fingerpicking guitar means unlocking the full potential of the acoustic guitar. Since you're reading this book, I bet that you already know that playing the acoustic guitar doesn't mean just strumming chords. While that's a useful technique, your instrument can offer much, much more than that.

When you start learning fingerpicking guitar, you will open the doors to new possibilities. It will allow you to pull off complex and beautiful arpeggio patterns, to play with more nuances than ever, to add percussion to your guitar playing, and most impressive, to play accompaniment and melodies at the same time.

These techniques will make you more resourceful than ever and can be incredibly useful for a wide variety of situations. They will help you in playing and coming up with better arrangements while playing with a band, which is useful in styles like Folk, Pop, and anything in between (even in Metal - think about songs like Metallica's Fade to Black or Nothing Else Matters). This will be especially useful if you're a singer-songwriter or play with one, since fingerpicking will allow you to play more interesting guitar parts.

Fingerpicking guitar can also turn you into a one-man-band who can play impressive solo guitar songs like Tommy Emmanuel or Don Ross. And as a nice side effect, learning fingerpicking guitar will allow you to play classical guitar pieces, which will expand your vocabulary further.

As you can see, the doors it opens are many and varied.

Yet from all the many guitar players in the world, only a few learn how to use its true potential. Those who do, however, are in the good company of guitarists like Merle Travis, Chet Atkins, or Andy McKee, just to name a few. These giants pushed and keep pushing the boundaries of what the acoustic guitar can do, and today we can stand on their shoulders to take our skills and music to a whole new level.

Join me in this journey, and together we'll discover the possibilities hidden within your guitar to help you make the best out of them.

Lastly, while my aim is to teach you how to play fingerpicking on an acoustic guitar, everything you'll learn here can also be played on an electric guitar. The sound and feel won't be the same though, so if you can, get hold of an acoustic.

Ready? Grab your guitar and let's start!

Guitar Tablature
What It Is and How to Use It

-Feel free to skip, if you already know how to read tabs

Let's clear up something right from the start:

**In order to master the guitar,
you do NOT have to learn how to read music.**

Yep. That's right. There are lots of famous guitarists that do not know how to read formal music. These include The Beatles, Eric Clapton, and Eddie Van Halen. However, I am not saying that learning to read music is a bad thing - quite the contrary. But it is true that you may well be able to reach your guitar-playing goals without needing to learn how to read countless pages of black lines with what looks like squashed ants all over the page.

To make things easier, in fact, MUCH easier, let's talk about an alternative way of noting (no pun intended) how to play the guitar. It's called "guitar tablature", or "tab" for short. It is similar to formal sheet music but it is far easier to understand, especially for beginner guitarists.

It looks like this (and by the way, this is a very famous melody!):

The top section shows formal music notation. But there is no need to concern yourself with that for now; in fact, you will often see guitar tab, where the music notation isn't there at all. However, it is very useful to have if you ever decide to take on learning how to read proper sheet music.

OK, now that's covered, let's take a good look at the lower section - the one that says "TAB" on it. You'll see that there are six lines that run horizontally across the page. Each of these lines represents one string of your guitar, with the line at the bottom representing the 6th string, and the line at the top representing the 1st string. Simple enough, right?

Therefore, when the guitar is on your lap, the string closest to you on the guitar (the 6th or Low (Thickest) E string) is the line closest to you on the TAB. And the string furthest from you on the guitar (the 1st or High (Thinnest) E string) is the line furthest away from you on the TAB. Some people do find this confusing at first, but it gets very easy, in a short amount of time with a little practice.

The numbers represent the frets that you are supposed to play the notes on. Even more simple!

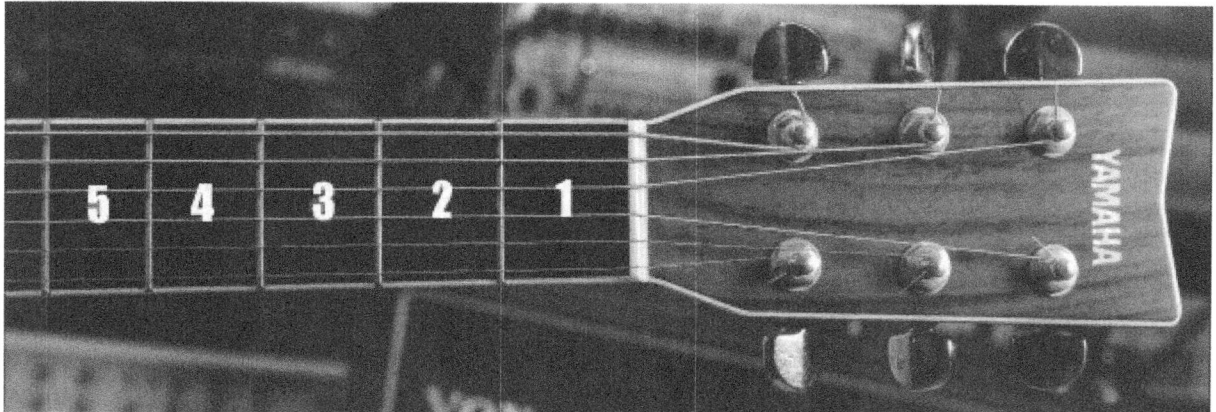

There are other elements of reading tab that are similar to music notation, such as time signatures and measures. No need to go into that now - let's just concentrate on getting the notes right first.

So, let's check it out the tab again:

If you read the tab correctly, you'll play the following notes one after the other..

- 4th string — 2nd fret (index)
- 4th string — 2nd fret (index)
- 4th string — 4th fret (ring)
- 4th string — 2nd fret (index)
- 3rd string — 2nd fret (index)
- 3rd string — 1st fret (index)

Now that you've played it does it ring a bell? Sounds like "Happy Birthday" to me - and it will to you too after you get it down pat!

If you want to get deeper into the world of tabs, we have a whole book dedicated to reading tabs. It will teach you everything you need to know about reading tabs and comes with a vast dictionary of guitar notation symbols.

And what's better – it's free!

You can get the free pdf here: www.theguitarhead.com/tabs

PART 1

FIRST 23 DAYS

Level 1

~ 2 days ~

Getting Started

The pima notation

Fingerpicking guitar is a lot about having good control on the fingers of your strumming hand (the right hand for most, the left hand if you're left-handed). It means learning how to move each one of your right hand fingers independently so that you can play two or more separate strings at the same time, as opposed to playing with a pick where you can play only one string or adjacent strings.

Since the use of the right hand fingers is at the core of fingerpicking guitar, most tabs use the pima notation, which we will also use in this book. This is a common notation for fingerpicking guitar that indicates which finger of your right hand should be used to play each note. Each finger is assigned one letter, each letter coming from the name of the finger in Spanish (that's because many influential early composers of classical guitar, the original guitar fingerpickers, were Spanish).

These are the letters associated with each finger and their original Spanish name:

$$\mathbf{P} = pulgar \text{ (thumb)}$$

$$\mathbf{I} = índice \text{ (index finger)}$$

$$\mathbf{M} = medio \text{ (middle finger)}$$

$$\mathbf{A} = anular \text{ (ring finger)}$$

Congratulations on completing your first Spanish lesson! Now back to fingerpicking: following the *pima* notation, a note with a *p* written on top of it means it has to be played with your thumb, a note with an *i* with your index finger, an *m* with your middle finger, and an *a* with your ring finger. Sometimes various notes have to be played at the same time; in this case, the letters will be written on top of each other.

Now, unless you're a Simpson's character or you've had an unfortunate Django Reinhard-type accident, you also have a pinky on your right hand. But the pinky is usually not used for picking the strings, and it's instead used for "anchoring" the right hand - more on this later. In the rare cases where the pinky is used to pluck a string, it's noted with the letter C or E.

The rule of thumb

As a general rule, string 1 is played by the ring finger (*a* in *pima* notation), string 2 by the middle finger (*m*), and string 3 by the index finger (*i*). Meanwhile, the thumb (p) takes care of strings 4, 5, and 6, all the lower strings. You will find various exceptions to this in this book and in the wild, but follow the *pima* notation and you'll be fine.

Part of the magic of fingerpicking guitar lies in that it sounds as if you're playing various instruments at the same time. Most times the notes played with the thumb will be like the bass in a band, while the rest of the fingers will play melodies and chords as a guitar normally does in a band. In addition, you can even add a "drumkit" to your one-man-band performance by slapping the strings with the thumb at the right moment. But we'll see more of that in later chapters.

The role of the thumb is the most important here. The secret to fingerpicking guitar is to get to control the thumb independently from the other fingers. It takes a bit of practice, but don't worry, with the exercises in this book you'll soon have it under control.

Right hand position

Let's start positive. Get in front of the mirror and give yourself a thumbs up. Now keep that hand posture and go back to the guitar, because that's how you'll get a good right hand posture.

Rest the left side of the thumb on the 4th string, and while keeping it there, rest the index finger (i) on top of string 3, the middle finger (m) on string 2, and the ring finger (a) on string 1. Now separate your hand from the strings so that you're not touching any. The knuckle of your middle finger (m) should be the furthest part of your hand from the guitar. In this position, try to pluck a string with the thumb. Make sure that you're able to pluck notes with the thumb without the other fingers getting in the way. This might sound difficult now, but try to keep your hand relaxed to avoid unnecessary tension.

Correct right hand position

And what about the pinky? Some players "anchor down" the pinky, some don't. Anchoring down the pinky means resting it near the edge of the sound hole to give you a point of reference and more stability. If you don't anchor it, your right hand will be "floating" on top of the strings.

Anchoring the pinky

Without anchoring the pinky

Anchoring or not comes down to personal preference, so try for yourself and see what feels more comfortable for you. If you anchor, try to keep the pinky relaxed so that you don't create unnecessary tension.

This might feel like a lot of information at once, but don't worry about getting it perfect right now. What matters is to keep improving bit by bit, to be even if just a tiny bit better than yesterday or last week.

Thumb exercises.

Let's start with a few exercises for the thumb.

We'll start with playing half notes on open low strings (meaning with no left hand fretting). Notice how the "p" below each note indicates that it should be played with the right hand thumb, according to the *pima* notation (Ex 1).

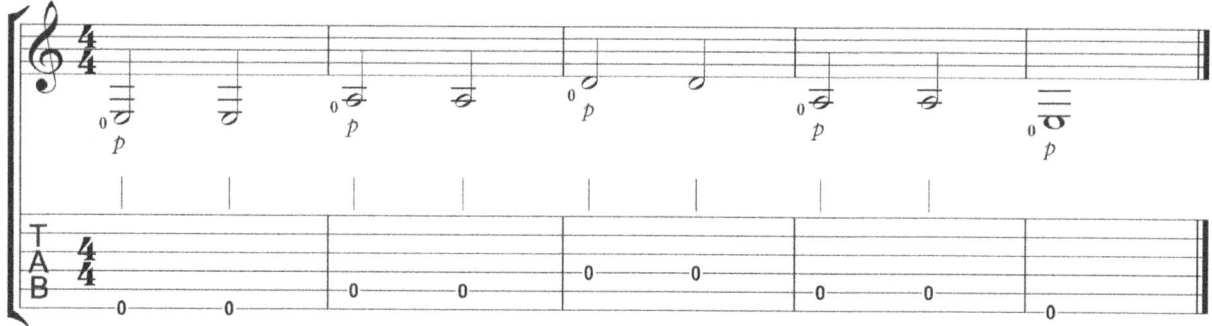

Well done. The next one includes a jump from string 6 to 4, which can be tricky if you're not used to control your thumb yet (Ex 2).

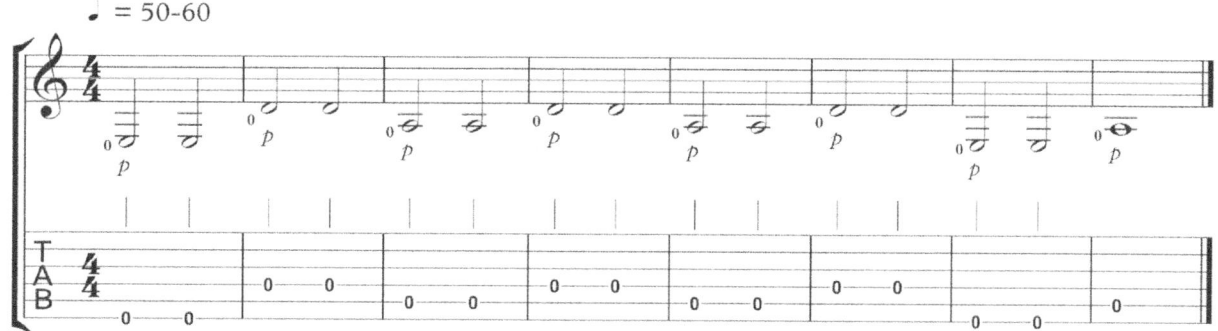

The next three exercises will make you gradually use the left hand to fret additional notes on the same strings (Ex 3).

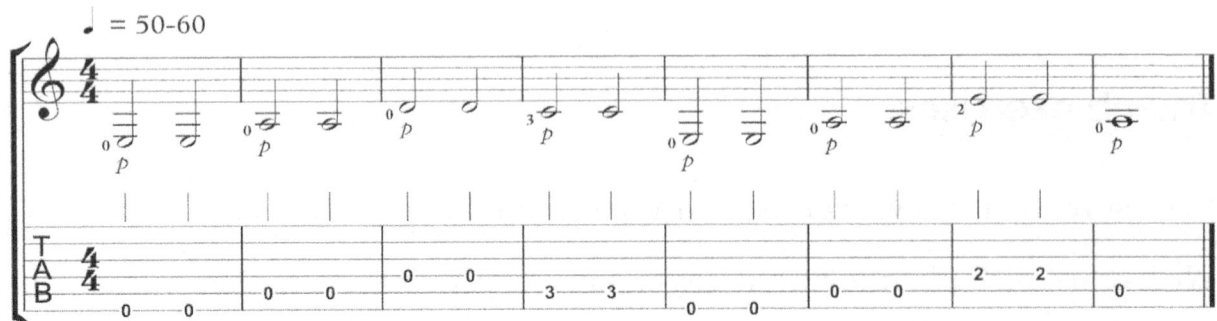

(Ex 4)

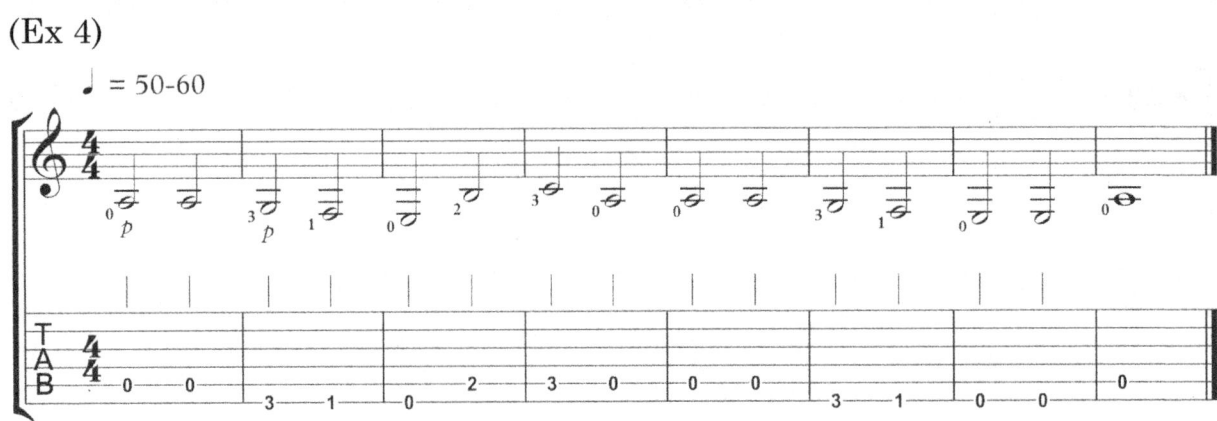

The next one is with quarter notes. Use a metronome to make sure you get it right (Ex 5).

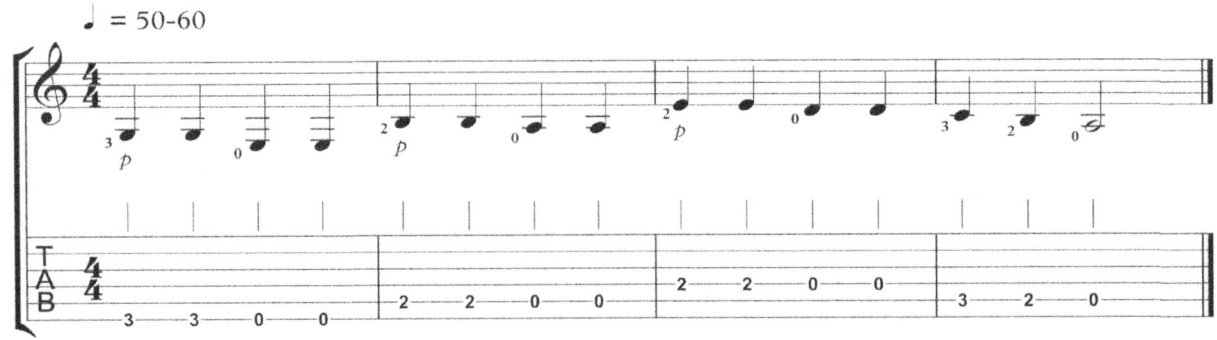

Now that we've warmed up that thumb, let's try the other right hand fingers. Let's start with the index finger (i) and middle finger (m). In the next exercises, you'll play a simple melody, each exercise will be different notes, on a different string.

To practice the use of different fingers, you'll see that here each note has two fingers assigned. First play following the upper letters (m, i, m, etc.) and then again following the lower letter (i, m, i, etc.).

Practicing with a metronome

For every exercise in this book, you'll see a recommended tempo value so that you can practice with a metronome. That's the best way to practice and I recommend you to try it. Start by playing the notes without it, taking your time for each note. Then try to play with a very low tempo value, like half of the recommended tempo or even less. We're practicing, so there's nothing as a too-slow tempo! If you can play it right, then increase the tempo and try again. Repeat this until you can play the exercise at the recommended tempo.

> **Note:** *If you don't have a physical metronome, there are plenty of free metronome apps and websites out there.*

Few more exercises

This exercise is all played on string 1 (Ex 6).

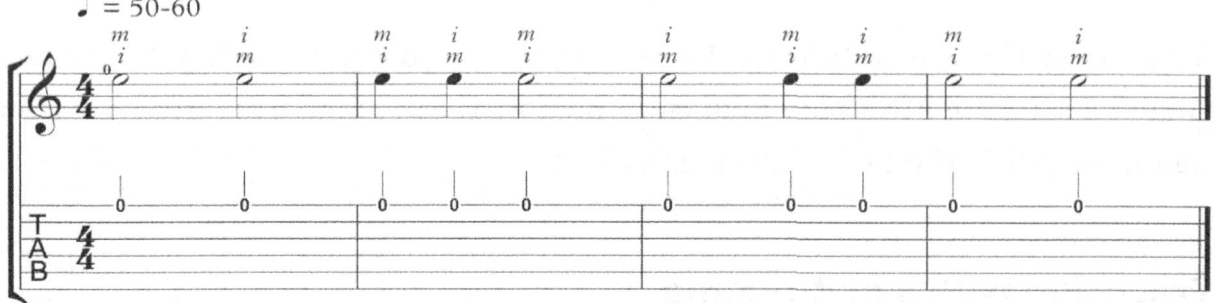

Now the same but on string 2 (Ex 7).

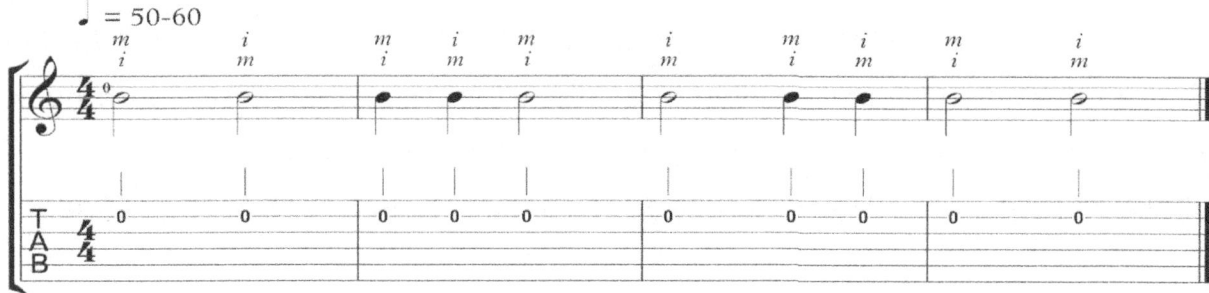

And now on string 3. Remember to play it first following the upper row of *pima* notation and then the lower row (Ex 8).

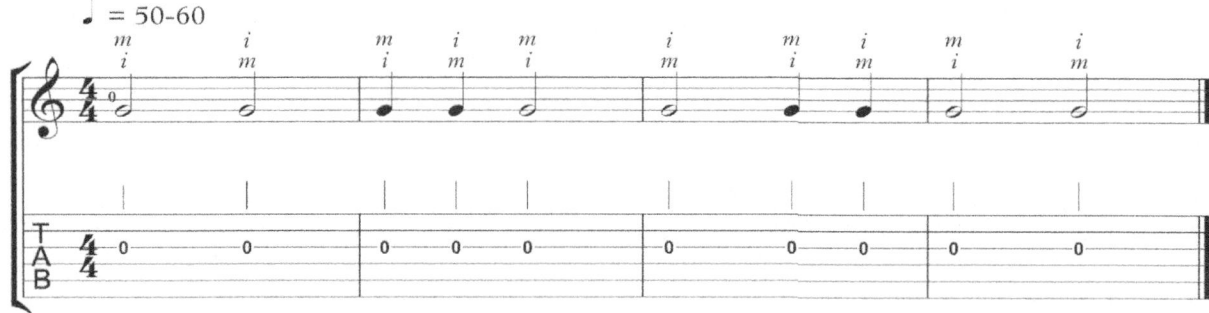

Let's increase the difficulty a bit. The next exercises use different strings within the same each one. You can let all strings ring; it's fine if they overlap, so you don't have to worry about stopping each note after playing it (Ex 9,10 & 11).

Let's add some left hand fretting. You can again let the open strings ring, but you don't need to keep the fretted notes ringing (Ex 12).

> **Note**: Audio tracks for these exercises are available in bonus section at the start of the book.

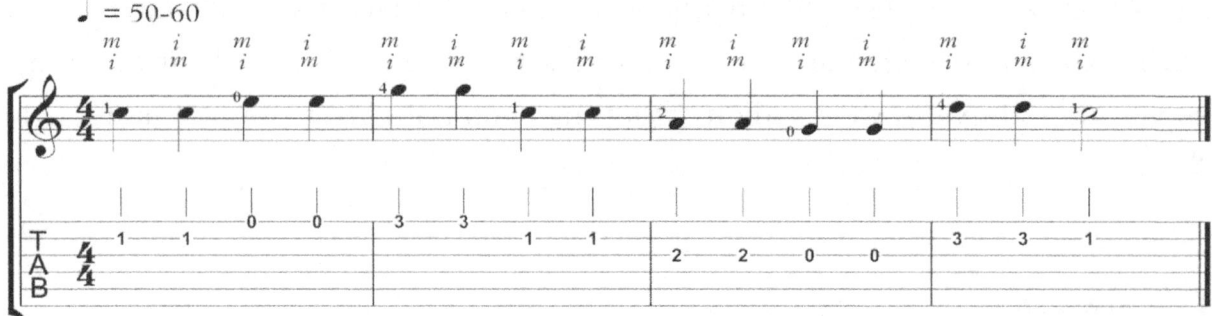

Now let's add the ring finger (a) into the equation. This is the most difficult finger of the four, so it's normal that it feels weird at first. Try to keep it relaxed, and take a break if it starts feeling uncomfortable.

The next exercises combine the *a* finger with the *i* and *m* fingers, one pair at a time (Ex 13, 14 & 15).

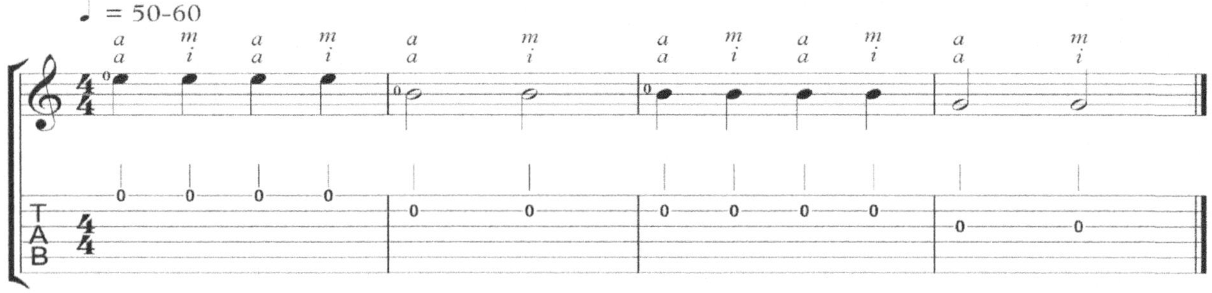

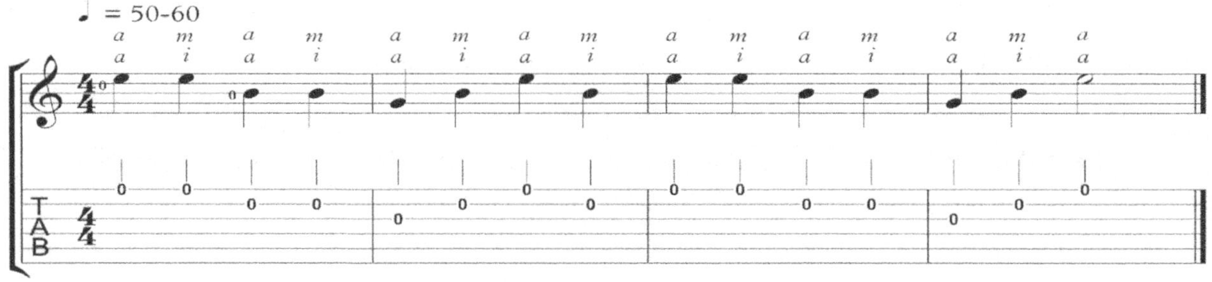

Now with left hand fretting. As usual, you can let open strings ring. Focus on playing each note with the correct right hand finger (Ex 16).

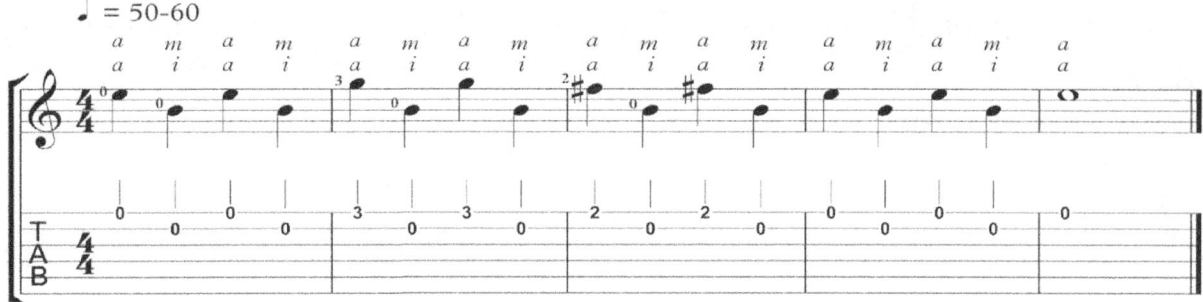

And now a combination of the three fingers at a time: i, m, and a. If you feel it's a bit confusing, it's normal. It takes a while to get used to using combinations of these fingers!

Let's start with half notes (Ex 17).

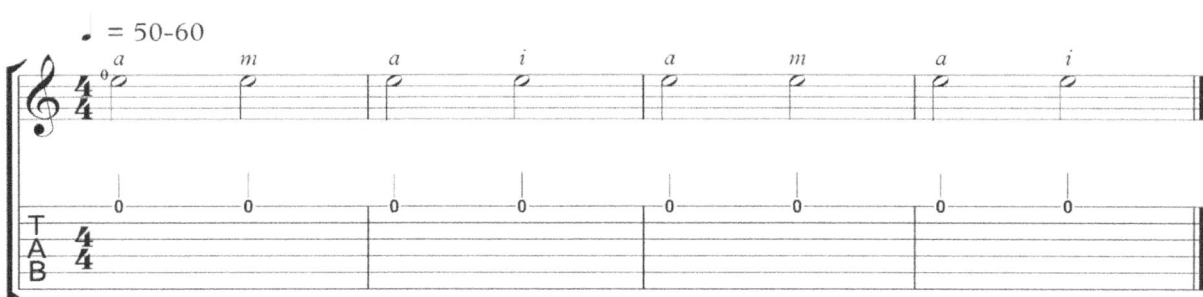

And now with also quarter notes (Ex 18).

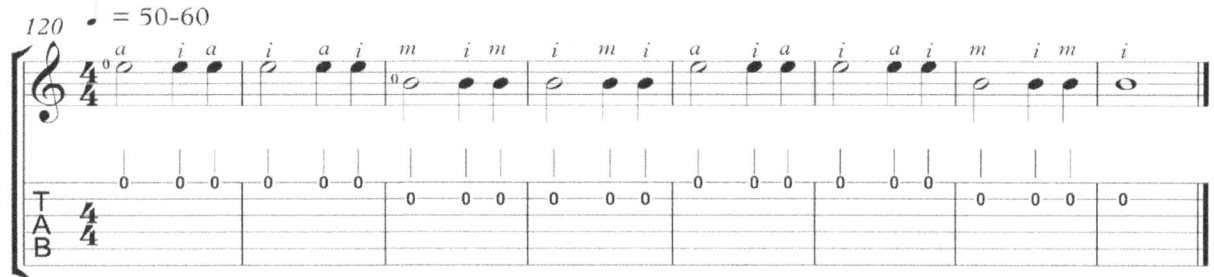

And now, using different strings within the same exercise. You see that the i finger always plays string 3, the *m* finger string 2, and the a finger string 1. This makes it easier to know which right hand finger to use. This is a common trend in many of the exercises and songs in this book (and outside of it too) (Ex 19).

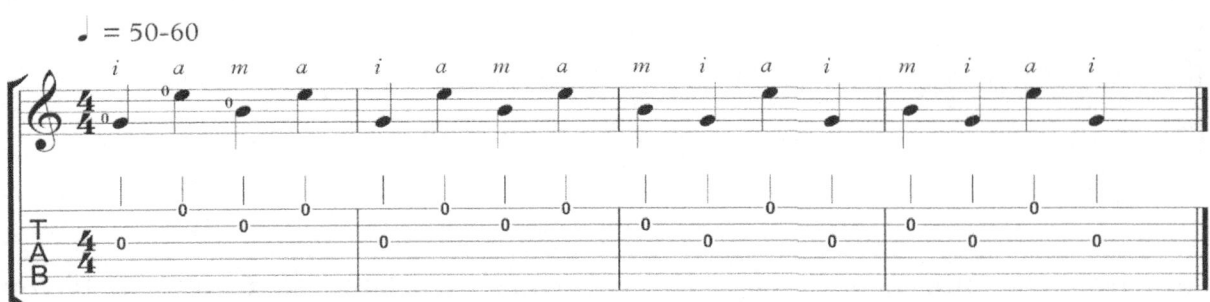

The following one has a 6/4 time signature, meaning with 6 beats per bar (Ex 20).

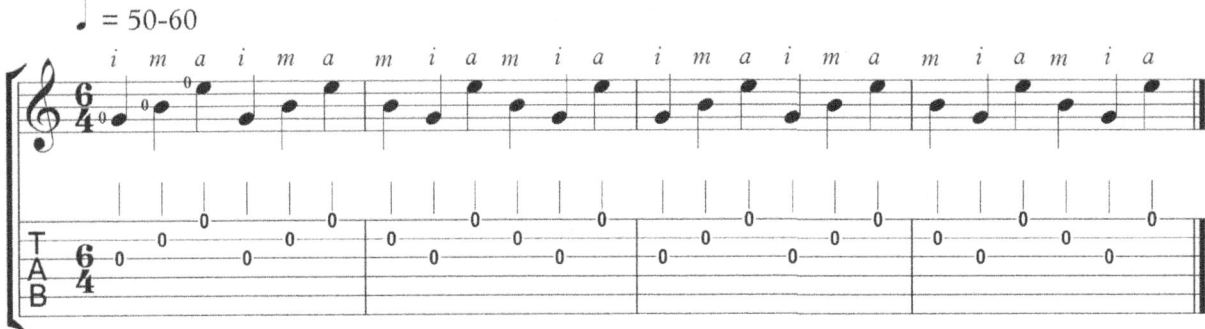

Commonly asked questions

Should I play with my fingertips or with my nails?

You can play with either, but the sound will be different with each. If you have very short nails and you pluck the strings only with the flesh of your fingertips, you will get a quiet, mellow sound. It can also be uncomfortable at first until you build up a bit of callous.

On the other hand (actually, on the same hand), playing with long nails will produce a louder and sharper sound. The problem is that if you don't have strong nails they can break easily. But even then, you can get acrylic nails that will allow you to play regardless of the natural strength of your nails. Also, having long nails on your strumming hand will signal that you're a badass fingerpicking guitar player, which will obviously earn you the admiration of those guitarists confined to the limitations of playing with a pick.

A common alternative is to have mid-length nails, no longer than 2-3mm, and pluck the strings with nails and a bit of flesh at the same time. This creates a good sound without the inconvenience of keeping your nails long.

And while we're on the topic, it's best to keep the nails on your fretting hand (left hand for most people) short so that they don't restrict your fretting.

Should I use nylon strings or steel strings?

Steel strings sound and crisp, while nylon strings have a more mellow sound. However, the choice will depend on the type of guitar: acoustic guitars are built for steel strings and classical guitars are built for nylon strings. Using the wrong type of strings will create a series of issues. For example, nylon strings aren't made to resist the tension the acoustic guitar needs, so if you use them on an acoustic guitar they will easily snap.

The type of guitar you choose depends on the genres of music you want to play, with classical guitar being the choice for Classical and Flamenco and acoustic guitar for most other genres.

Should I use a thumbpick?

A thumbpick is like a half-ring, half-pick, attached to your right hand thumb, which allows you to play as if you had a pick while freeing the other four fingers on your right hand. Playing the thumb notes with a thumbpick instead of the flesh of your thumb provides a more powerful sound with more attack and clarity.

Yet perhaps the most interesting part of using a thumbpick is that it allows you to switch between fingerpicking and flatpicking (playing with a pick) on the fly. This allows you to combine the best of both worlds: the flexibility and nuances of fingerpicking with the speed and precision of flatpicking. Check out Tommy Emmanuel playing live and you'll see what I'm talking about.

But before running out to the music store to get a bunch of thumbpicks, keep in mind that it takes time to get used to it. And until you do so, it can be quite uncomfortable. Because of this, I recommend you to go through this book playing with your bare fingers, and then later you can decide to give thumbpicks a try or not.

Conclusion

Congratulations on finishing the first level! You've learned the foundation of fingerpicking guitar, you've used your right hand fingers for the first time, and you've even had an unexpected Spanish lesson.

See you in the next level!

Level 2

 3 days

Finger Team Work

It's time to introduce your thumb to the rest of your fingers. As I explained in the previous level, in fingerpicking guitar the role of the thumb is often different than the other fingers - it often moves around more than any of the other right hand fingers and it's important to be able to move it freely.

However, this movement has to be coordinated with the movement of the other fingers. This is what we'll practice in the following exercises.

In this first one, the thumb jumps from string to string while the other fingers keep playing string 1 every second note (thumb, another finger, thumb, another finger, etc.). There are three rows of *pima* notation: play the exercise three times, one for each row. Two of them alternate between index finger (i) and middle finger (m) on string 1, while the third is all with the index finger (i). All notes are played on open strings - the left hand isn't used at all so that you can focus on the right hand. You can let all strings ring.

Feel free to go back to level1 to check the letters associated with each finger anytime you need it (Ex 1).

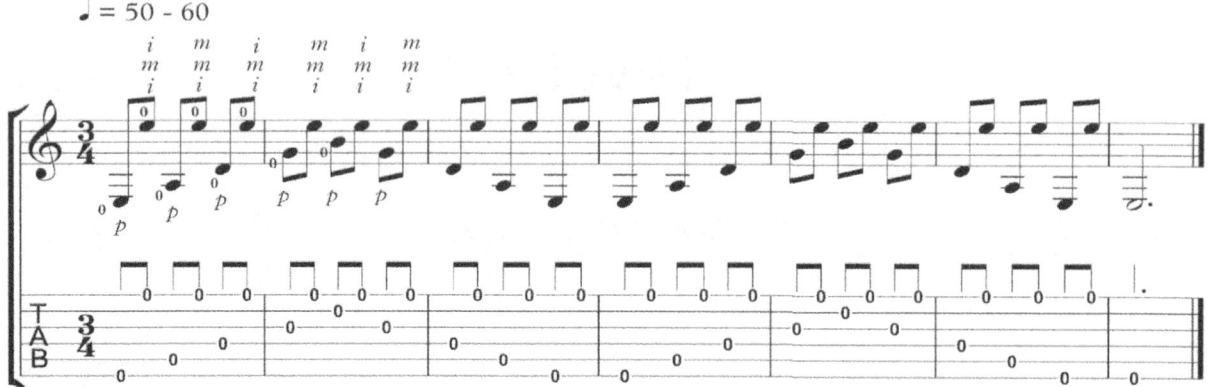

Here comes a similar exercise, but this time the thumb stays on one string while you use the other fingers to play each time a different string. Pay attention to the *pima* notation to know which finger to use each time (Ex 2).

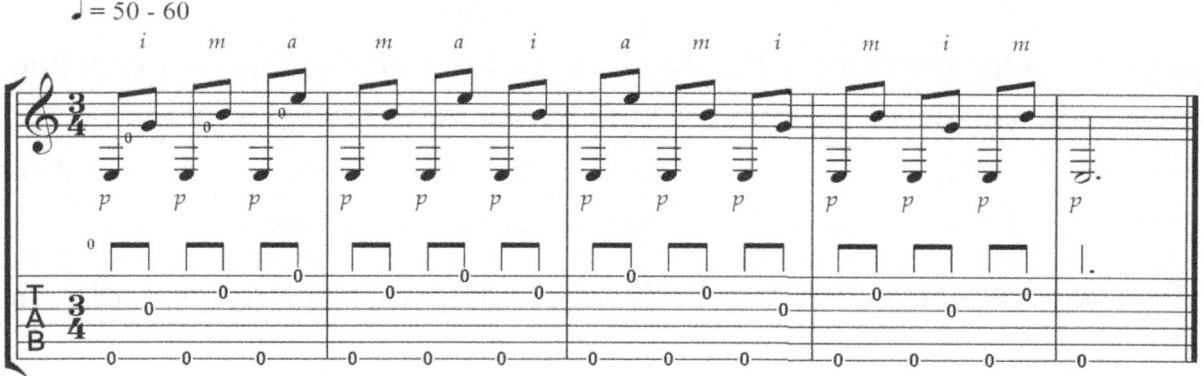

Now let's try a bit of both: first some movement with the thumb and then with the other fingers (Ex 3).

> **Note** : Refer audio tracks in the bonus section to understand how it should sound.

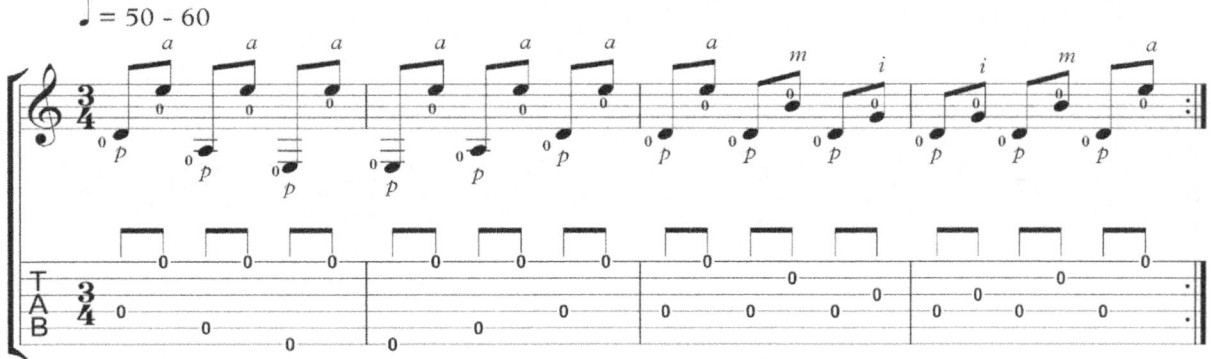

(Ex 4)

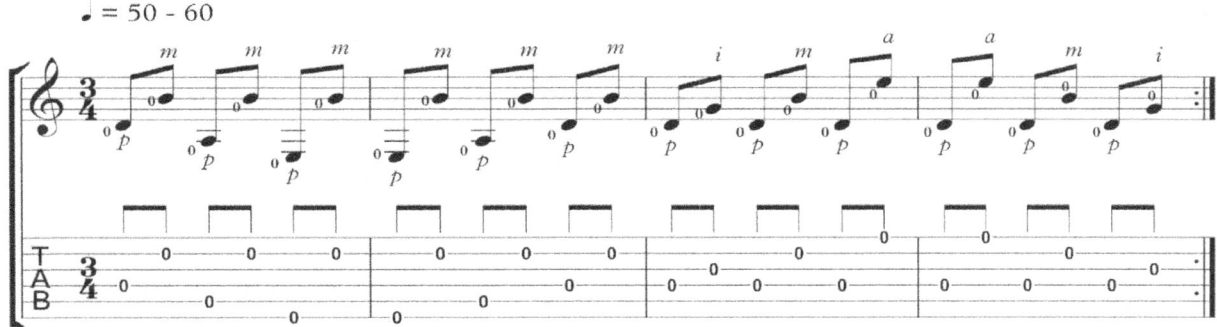

(Ex 5)

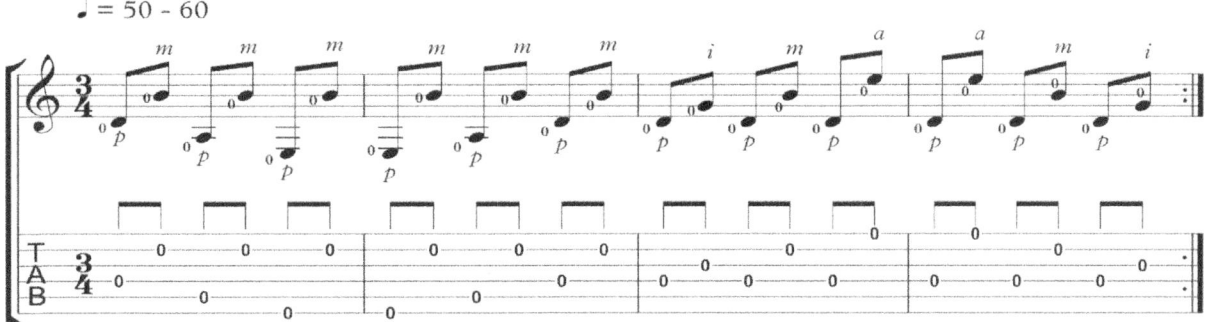

Time to try something new: until now you've played notes one finger at a time, in succession. In the next exercises, you'll play with the thumb at the same time as other fingers (Ex 6 & 7).

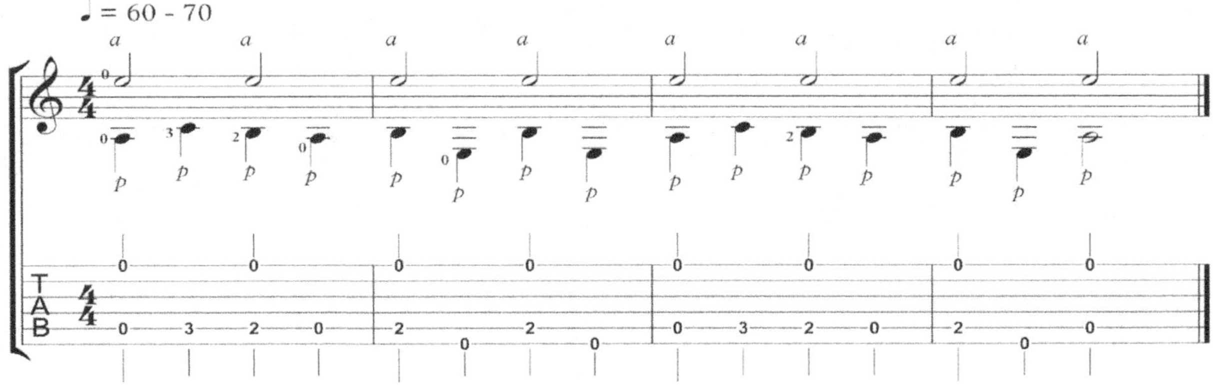

Fingerstyle guitar

The next one is in a 3/4 time signature, with 3 beats per bar (Ex 8 & 9).

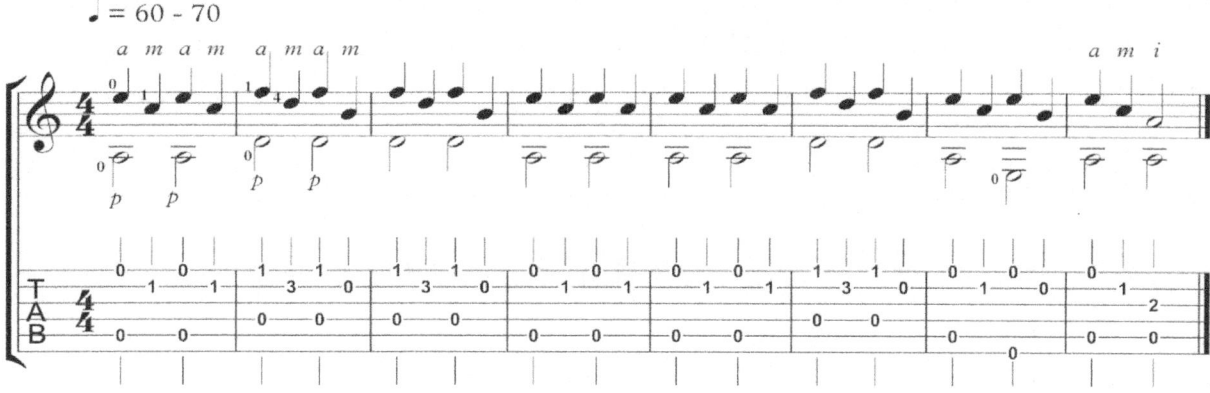

Here you'll play more than one fretted note at once. If you fret all the left hand notes in the first or third bar at once, you'll notice it's the fingering C chord. You can keep that position for the duration of the whole bar while your right hand plucks the notes. In the same way, bars two and four have the left hand fingering of a G chord (Ex 10).

In fingerpicking guitar, it's also common to see combinations of index (i), middle (m), and ring (a) fingers playing together. Playing various strings at the same time can often feel confusing at first, so I recommend you to start playing each exercise very slow. Once you can play slowly, increase the speed gradually until you can play it at the tempo specified at the top of each exercise. The metronome is your friend!

In this exercise, let the low strings ring. Because the higher strings are mostly fretted, they will stop ringing the moment you change your left hand fingering (Ex 11).

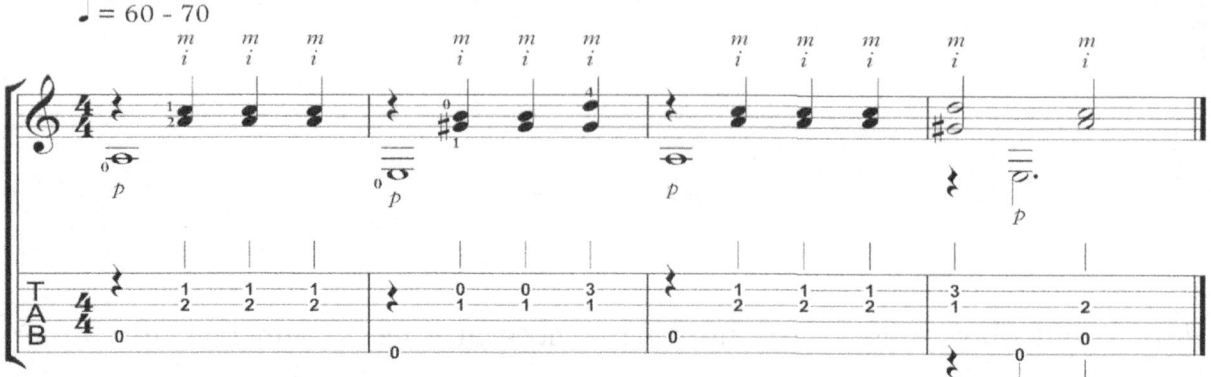

In this one, try to let all the open strings ring (Ex 12).

In many finger picking tabs and music sheets you'll find that you can let the notes ring longer than its written, especially when it comes to open strings. Again, try to let all open strings ring here (Ex 13).

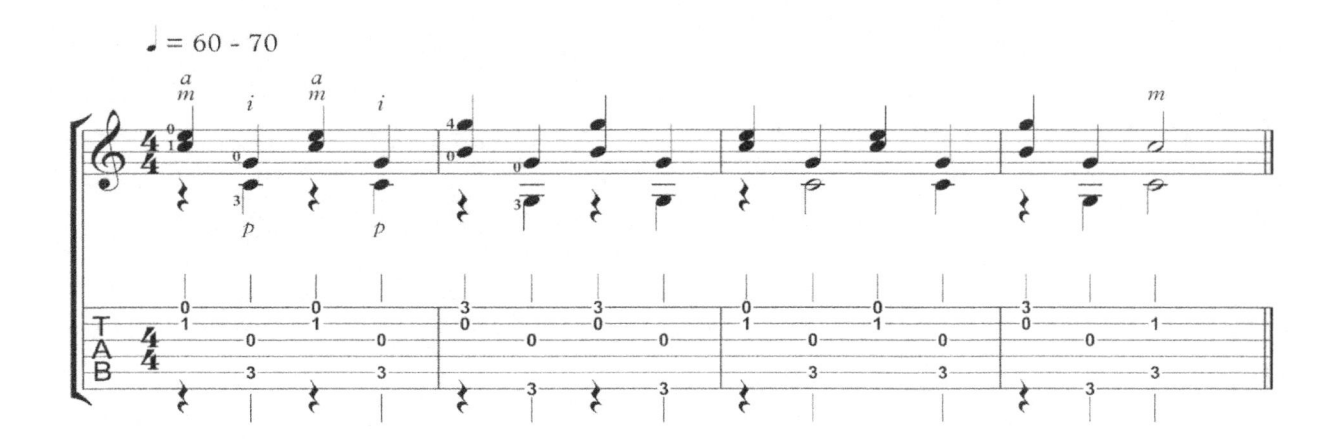

Now let's go back to alternating strings. This time the thumb will start as high as string 2 while middle (m) and index (i) fingers alternate between each other on string 1. Try to let string 1 ring for the whole exercise (Ex 14).

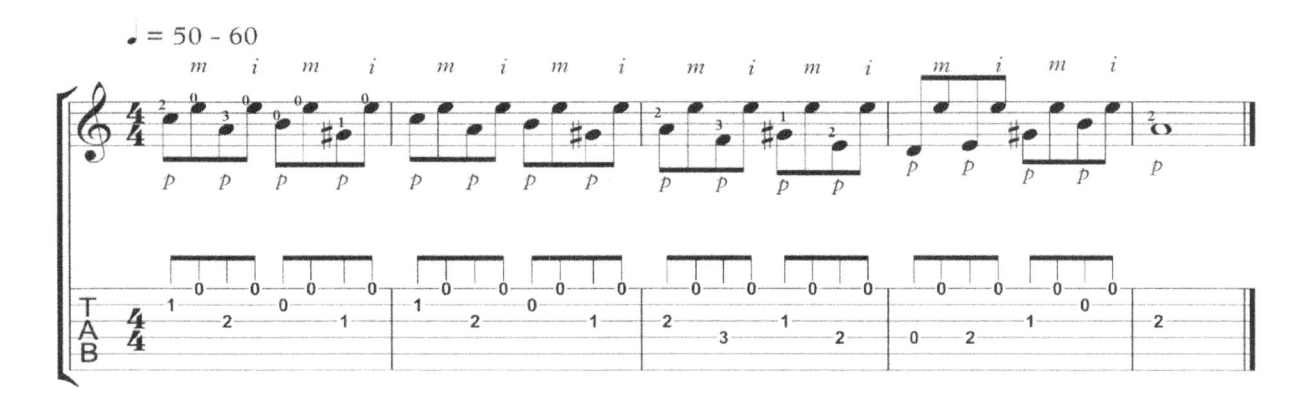

The next exercises use triplets (three notes per beat). In the first two, the thumb notes fall on the beat all the time, use that to help you keep the rhythm (Ex 15 & 16).

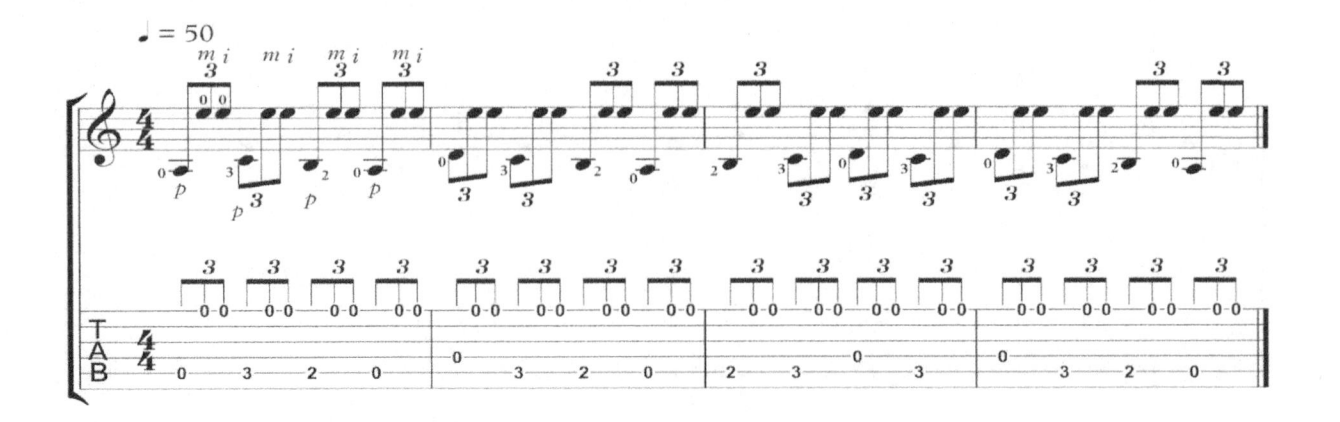

To finish the level, let's play two exercises in which the thumb won't be playing on the beat, making it a bit more tricky to keep the rhythm. Start very slow and use that metronome to keep you in rhythm (Ex 17 & 18).

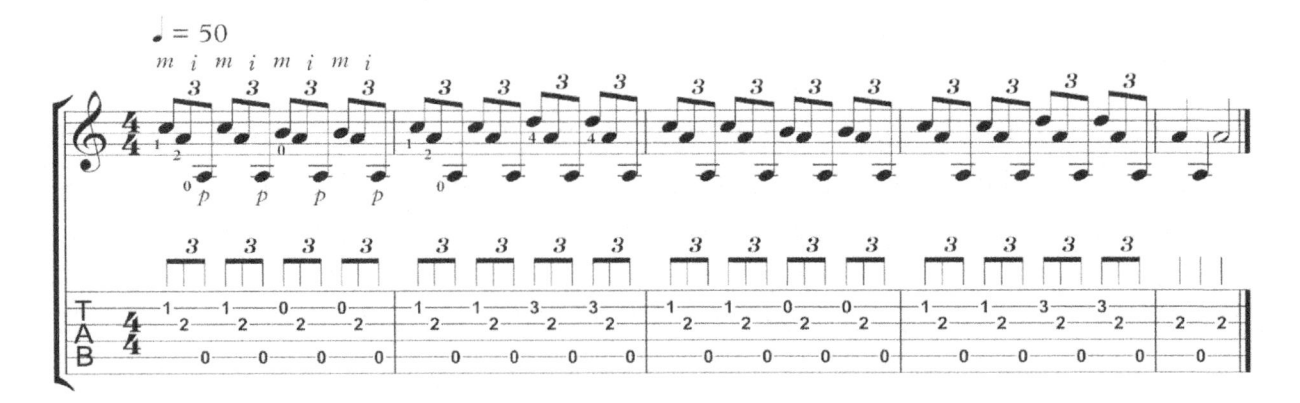

Conclusion

Good job! In this level, we've improved the coordination of your right hand fingers. Take a moment to congratulate them on their teamwork! Yet at this point, it's normal if you still don't feel confident with them. Everyone feels clunky at first, and we're just getting started. What matters is not doing it perfectly, but getting a tiny bit better with each step. If you feel overwhelmed, take a break, and when you come back to it play the exercises very, very slowly. Focus on getting it right first; speed will come later.

When you feel ready, jump to the next level and you'll see how things start making more sense.

Level 3

~ 3 days ~

Arpeggios

Here's a little secret about fingerpicking guitar: Every time you see a tab that looks complex, it's very possible that it's just a normal chord being arpeggiated following a pattern.

Arpeggiating a chord means playing it string by string, note by note, instead of strumming or plucking all strings at once. For example, the typical C chord on a guitar is made of different notes (C on string 5, E on string 4, G on string 3, a C an octave higher on string 2, and an E an octave higher on string 1). When you strum a chord you play all these notes at once. But when you *arpeggiate* it, you play it note by note, usually following a pattern.

Patterns

An arpeggio pattern is simply a way to arpeggiate a chord with the right hand. For example, for the previous C chord, a possible pattern could be plucking first C, then G, then E, then the higher C, and repeat. This is just one of the many, many patterns that you can play on a single chord.

The magic of arpeggio patterns lies in that the same pattern can be used on almost any chord you want. This makes them an incredibly efficient way of learning since one single pattern can often be used on a ton of different songs.

Enough talking, let's play! The next exercises will show you some arpeggio patterns. Finger the chord written on each with your left hand and keep it there, as if you were about to strum the chords. But instead of strumming with your right hand, play each separate note with the appropriate finger as indicated with the *pima* notation. The first pattern is simple and ascending, using all four fingers, one after the other. The first beat of every bar falls on the thumb here (Ex 1).

The second one skips a string after the thumb note. The second half is similar to the first one, but with all fingers except the thumb on strings 1 and 2 instead of strings 2 and 3 (Ex 2).

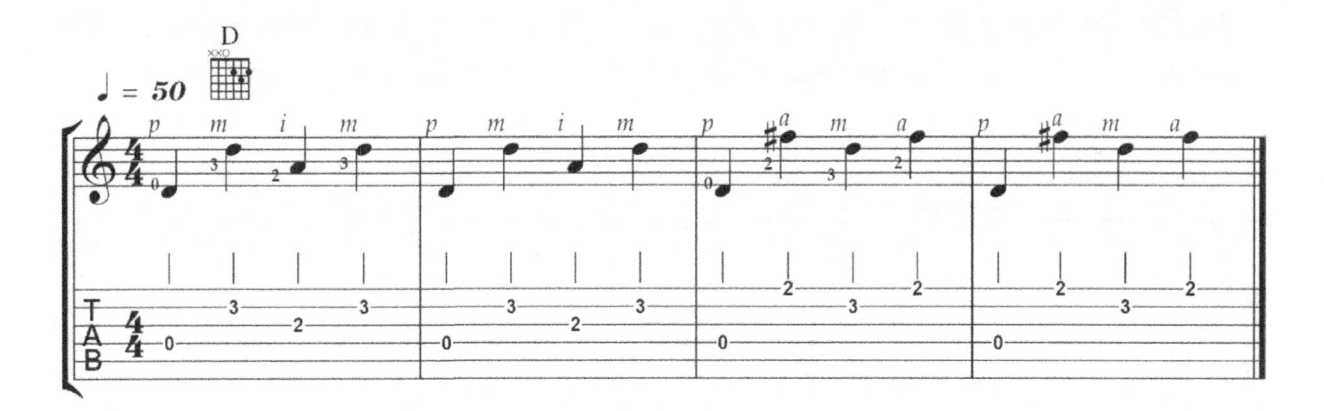

This arpeggio pattern goes up and down. You'll find a similar pattern in a lot of modern music, for example in *Every Breath You Take* by The Police (Ex 3).

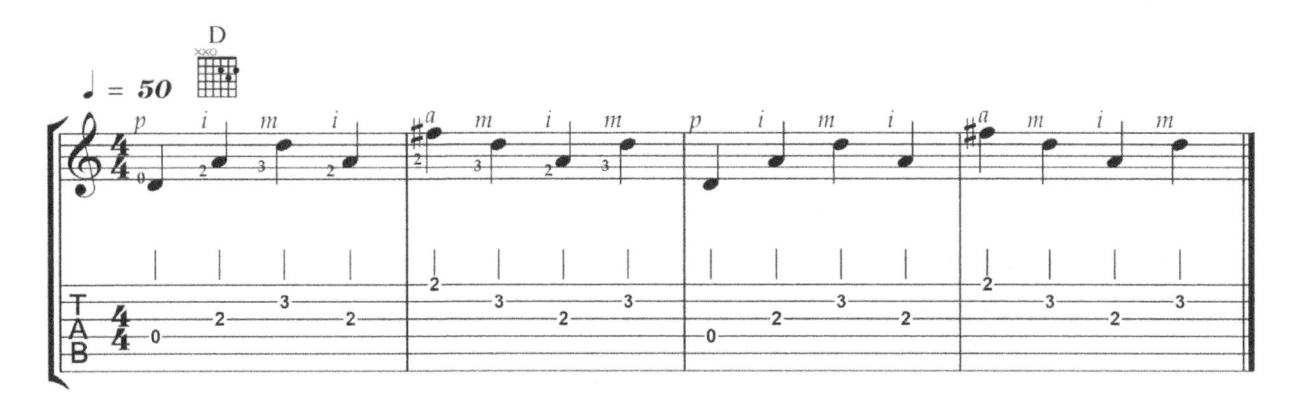

The fourth pattern introduces eight notes. Use a metronome to make sure you play it right, without dragging or rushing (Ex 4).

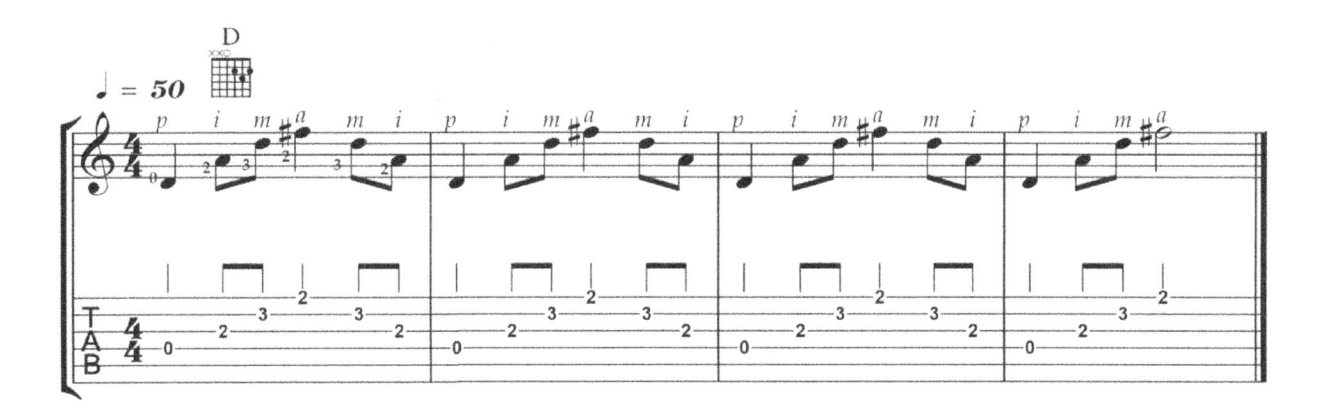

Fingerstyle guitar

And the fifth and last one is fully in eight notes. Every beat falls on the thumb, use this (and a metronome) to help you keep the rhythm (Ex 5).

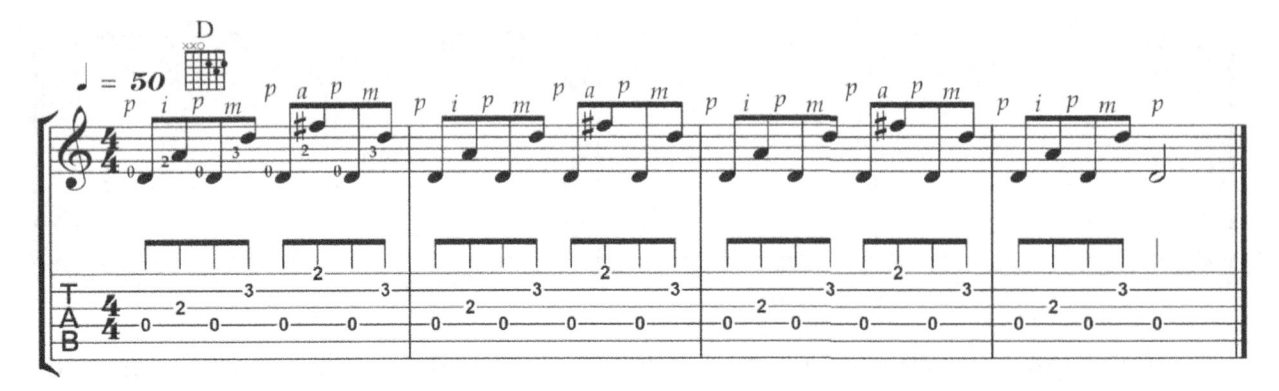

> **Note** : Audio tracks for these exercises are available in bonus section at the start of the book

To show you how the same pattern can be used on different chords with (barely) any changes on the right hand movements, the following exercises are the patterns you've just played but on the A chord instead of the D chord.

Notice how we start on a different string, as if all notes have moved down one string. The idea is to start with the root note of the chord: while the patterns on the D chord start on string 4 (D string), the same patterns on an A chord start on string 5 (A string). Once translated to the different strings, the movements of the right hand fingers are the same. This means that if you could play the previous patterns on a D chord, you shouldn't have problems playing them on an A chord, or practically on any other chord for that matter (Ex 6-10)

Arpeggios

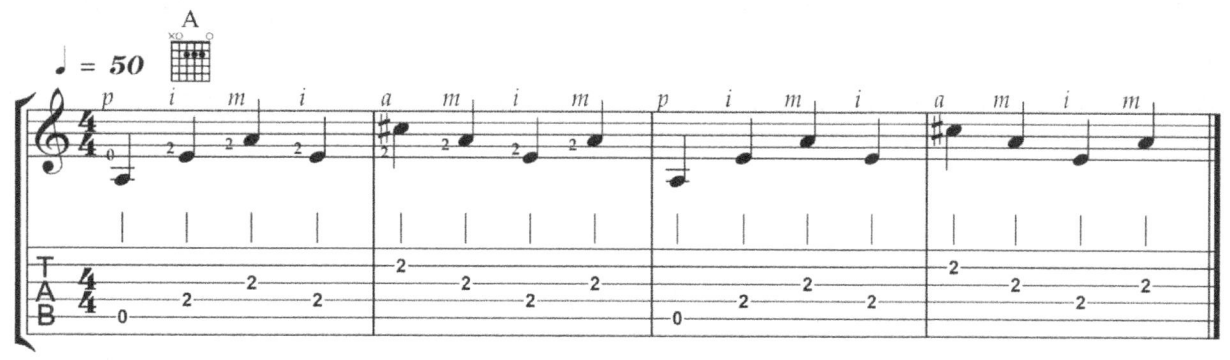

Fingerstyle guitar

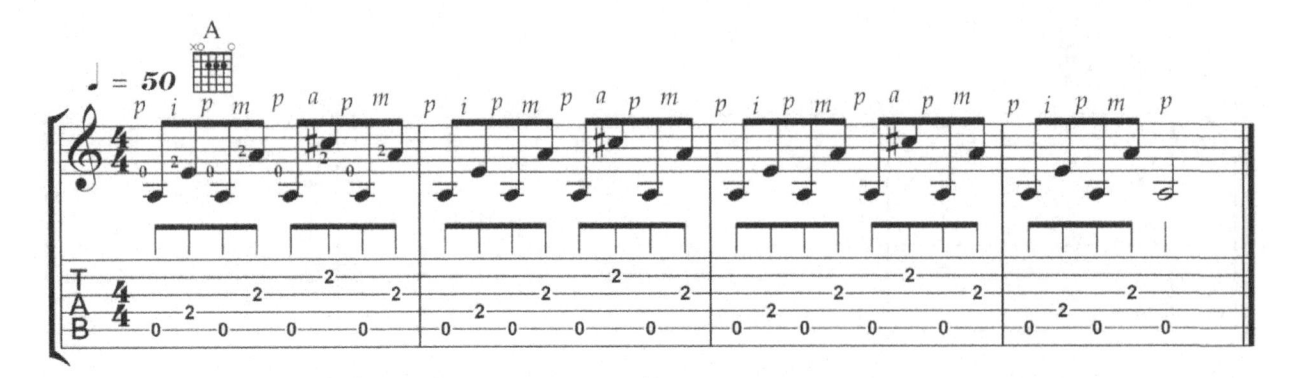

And now let's try to play the same pattern again, but now on a G chord. This time the thumb will start on string 6 (starting with a low G note) while the other fingers stay on the same strings as when we played the A chord. The order in which you pluck the strings is the same, the only thing that changes is the string your thumb will pluck.

While you could change the position of the other fingers one string lower, keeping them on higher strings sounds better in this case. If in the future you want to come up with your own arpeggio patterns, with time you'll start to recognize which combinations of strings sound best when playing each chord (Ex 11-15).

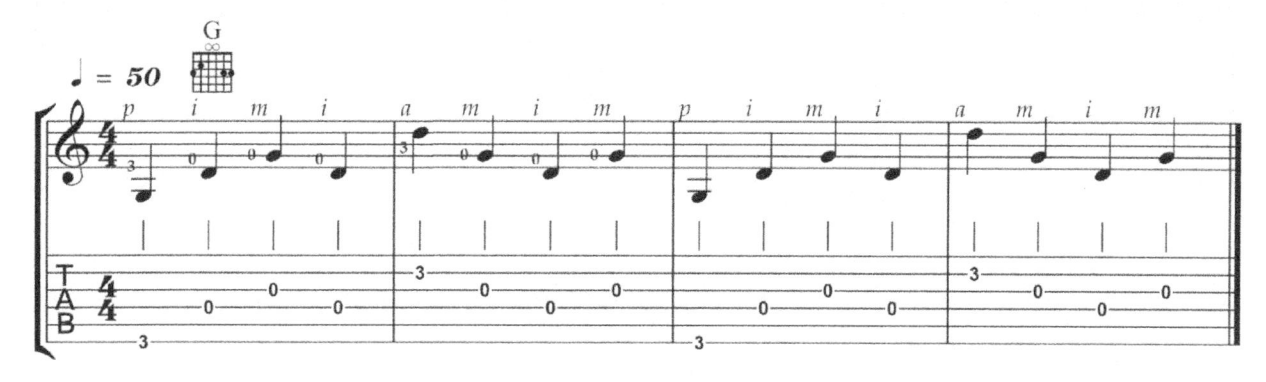

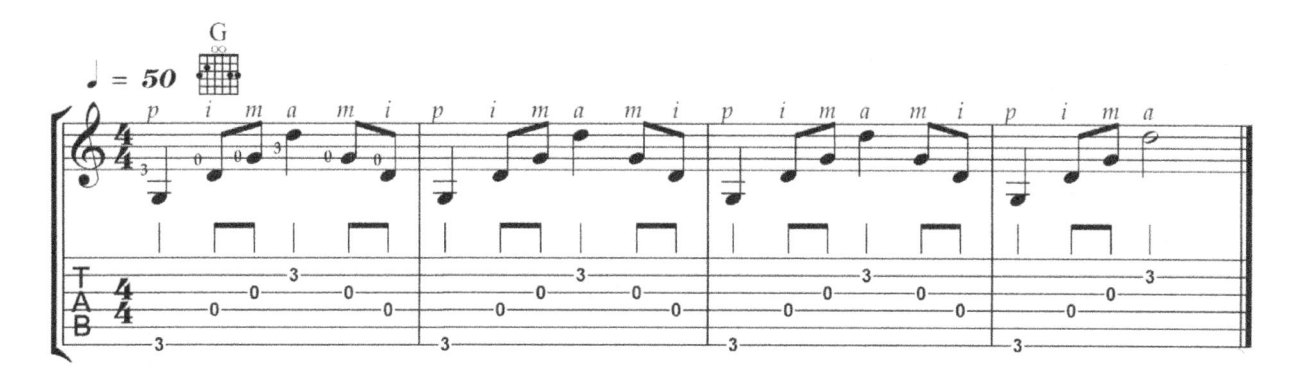

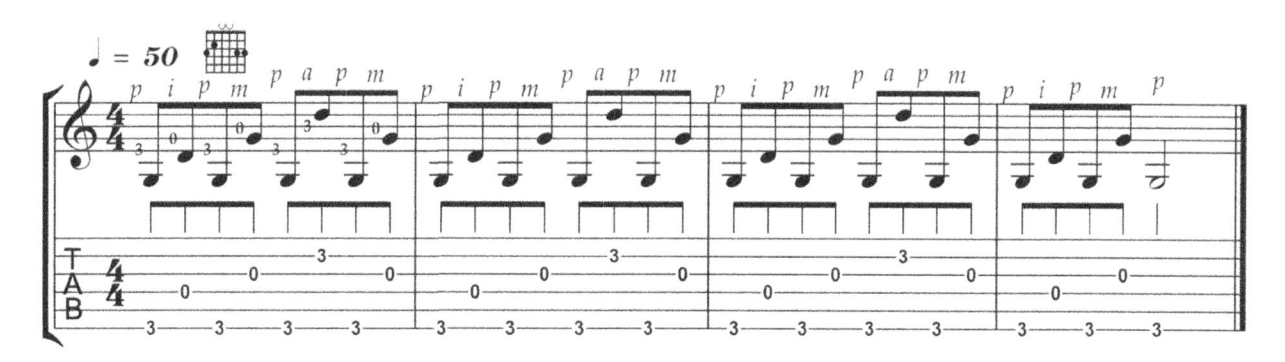

Arpeggios

Good job! Now let's try changing chords within the same exercise. In the next one, you'll switch between the A and D chords, while the right hand plays a similar pattern each time (moving it all one string down for A and then back up for D) (Ex 16).

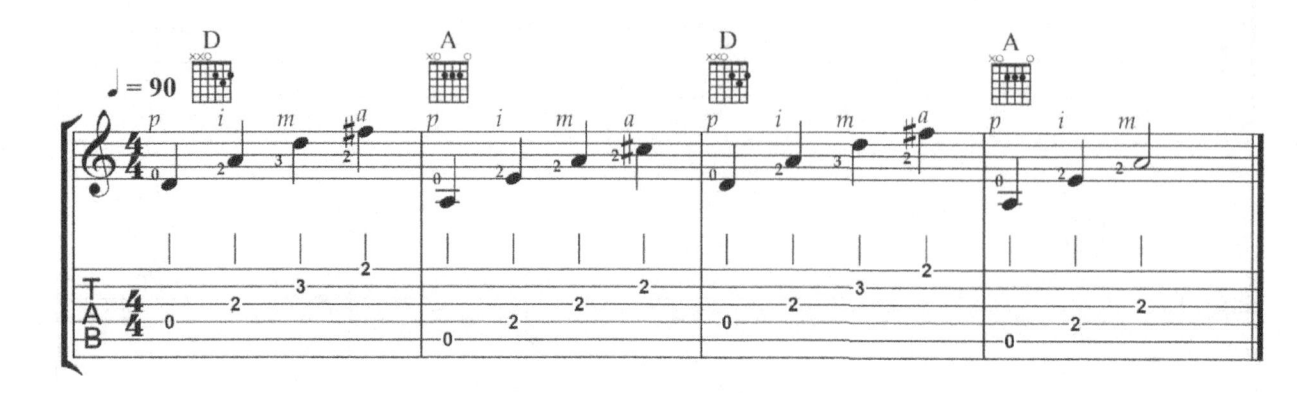

Now a different pattern and switching between G and C. Notice how, in the right hand, only the thumb changes strings while the rest of the fingers stay on the same string. Pay attention to the time signature of 6/4, meaning there are 6 beats per bar (Ex 17).

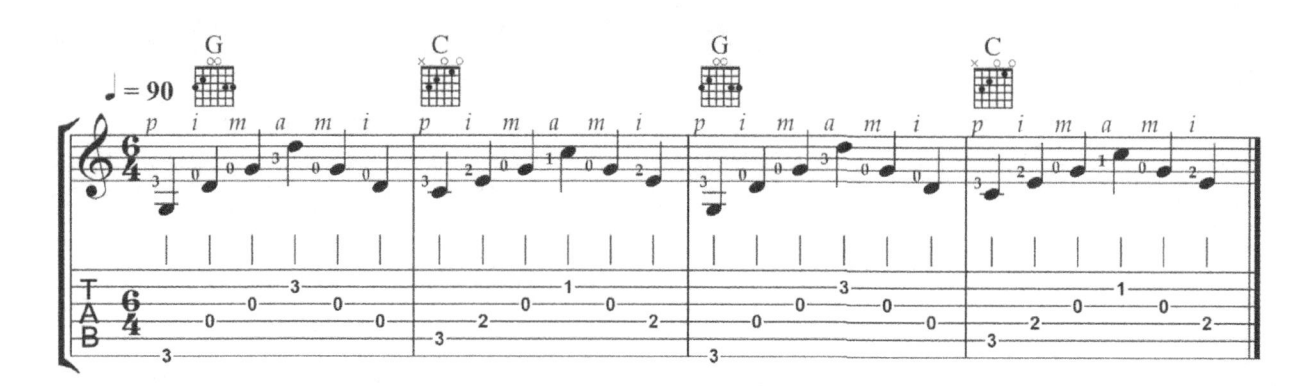

Most of the time, arpeggios patterns start with the root note of the chord, but that's not always the case. In this exercise, the C chord starts on the E note (2nd fret on string 4) instead of on C (which would be the 3rd fret on string 5), making it an "inverted" chord (Ex 18).

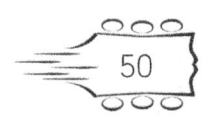

Arpeggios

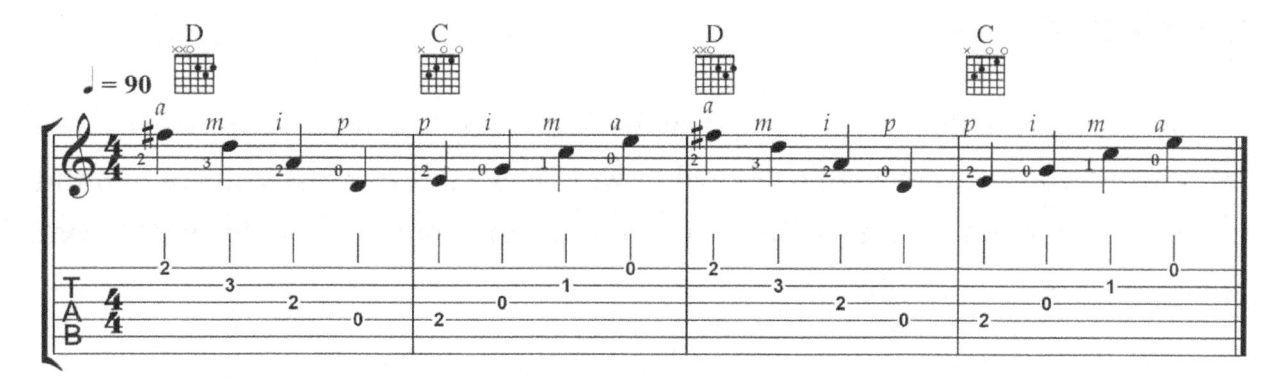

Now let's try to combine different chords on a pattern that uses two strings at the same time. Notice that the first G chord has a slightly different fingering than the last one. Both are still a G, it's just different ways of playing the same chord. Choosing to use one or the other often comes down to personal taste, but I've added both here just to confuse you. Sorry, I meant "to expand your knowledge" (Ex 19).

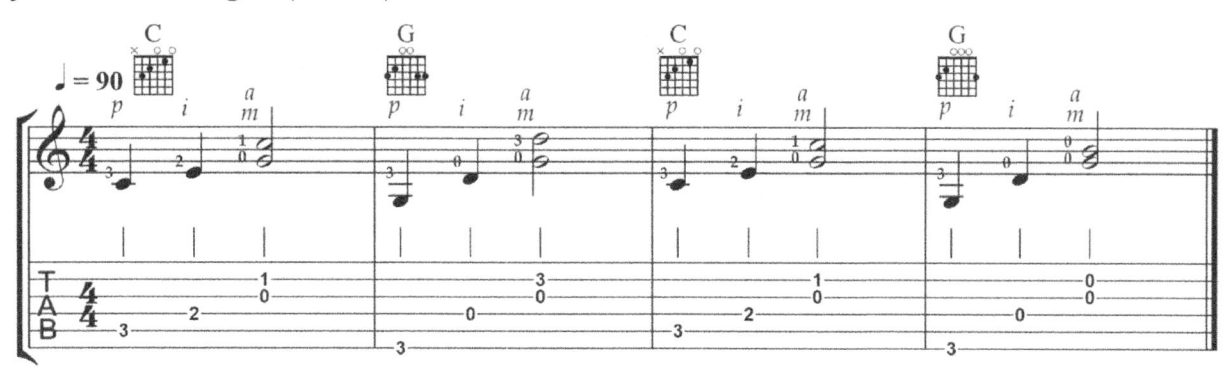

To finish this level, here goes another exercise on a 6/4 time signature (Ex 20).

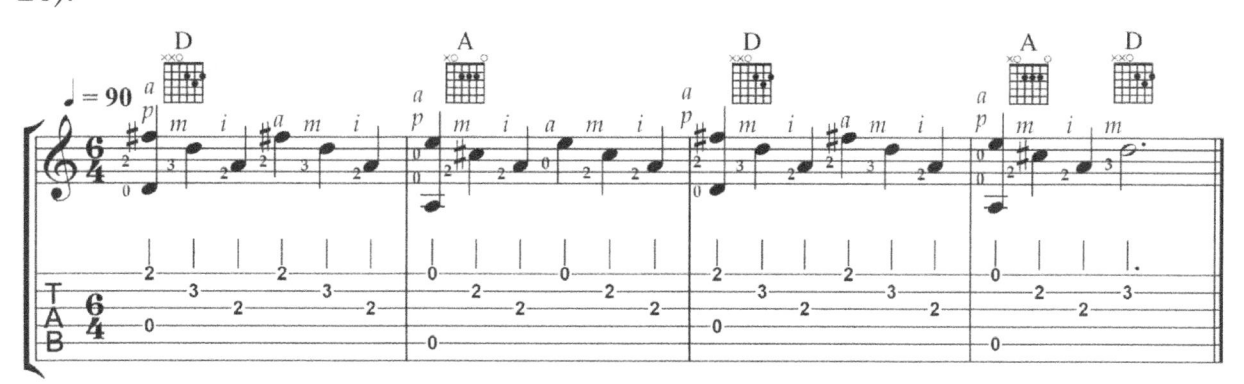

Conclusion

You're at the end of level 4. We've unveiled the magic of arpeggio patterns and its power - you're an arpeggio wizard now, Harry. You can use your newfound pattern powers on practically any chord you want, but remember: with great power comes great responsibility.

See you on the next level, where we'll start playing real songs.

Hasta la vista, baby.

Level 4

∽ 3 days ∽

Getting Ready For The Real World

I have good news for you. In the previous level, we tested various arpeggio patterns, made for you to practice. And it might have looked just like just that, isolated practice. But truth is that if you could play the exercises in the previous level, you're already able to play many, many songs. Sure, we're not at the level of Tommy Emmanuel or Chet Atkins yet. But in the context of songwriter or band songs, you can already do a lot.

So in order to make you see how far you've already made it, in the next exercises we'll take two different arpeggio patterns and apply them over the chords of well-known songs. The results will be something that you could play with a singer or a band, or even record on an album if you can play it well with the recommended tempo (for real).

Let's start with "Knocking on Heaven's Door". Originally by Bob Dylan, it's been covered by many artists, with Guns and Roses' version probably being the most known, especially among guitarists. But we're not here to emulate

Slash (you're reading the wrong book for that), we're here to turn those easy chords into beautiful arpeggiated goodness.

As in some of the previous exercises, the thumb is the only finger that jumps from string to string (Ex 1).

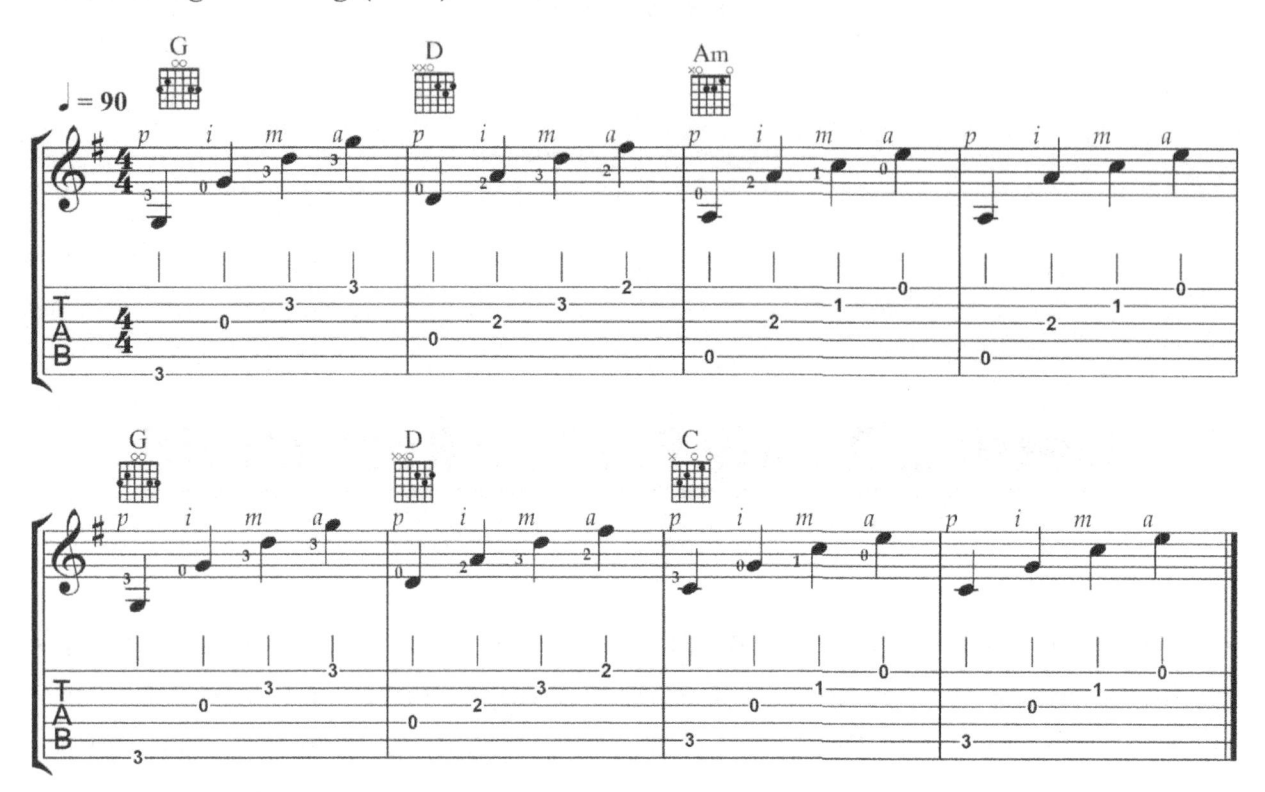

And now let's try the exact same chords with a different pattern. Notice how the tempo of this exercise is lower. Use a metronome to get it right; start very, very slow, and when you can play it right dial it up a bit and repeat. Keep doing until you can play it at 60bpm! (Ex 2)

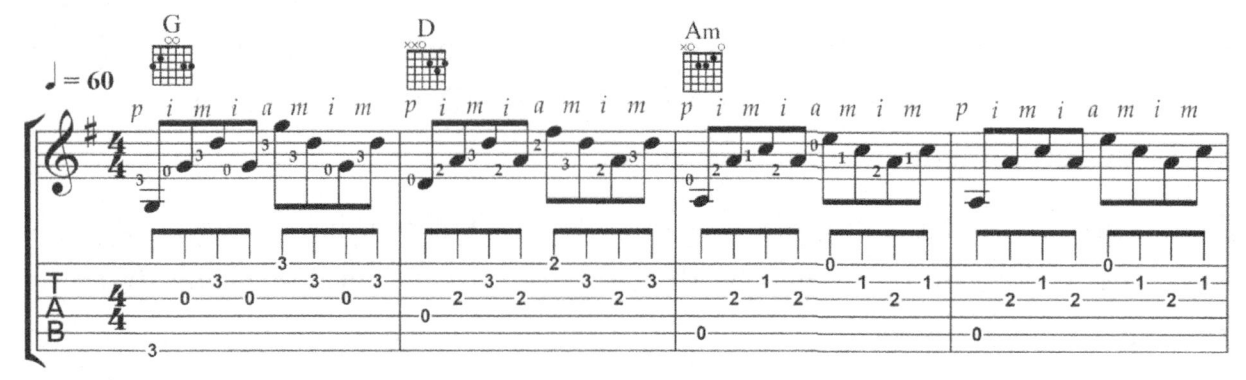

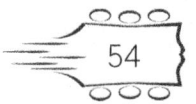

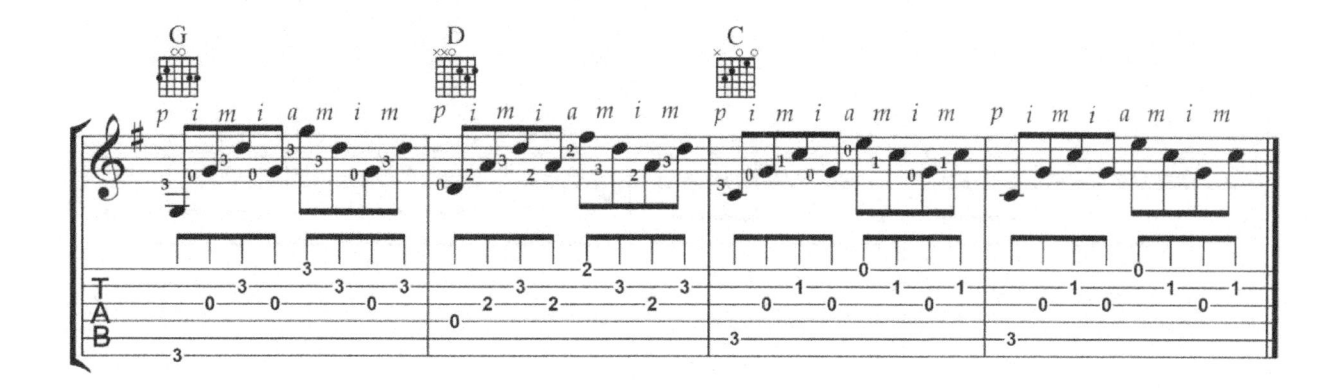

Now a different chord progression. These are the chords of the chorus of "Take Me Home, Country Roads" by John Denver, an iconic country song. Again, the same chords played on two different patterns (Ex 3 & 4).

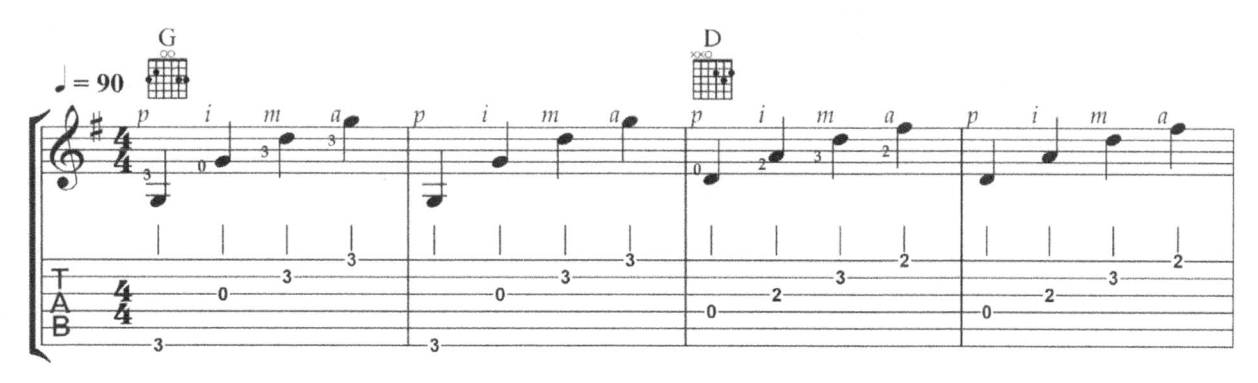

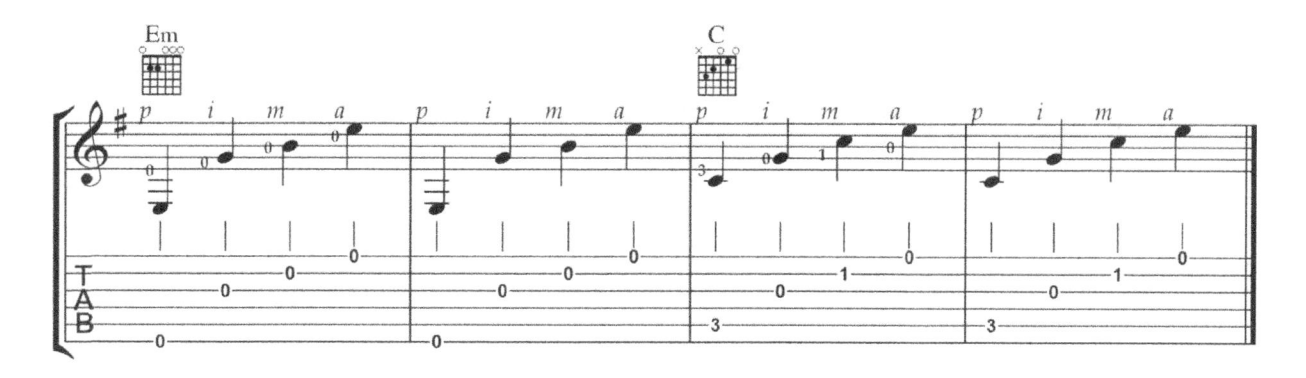

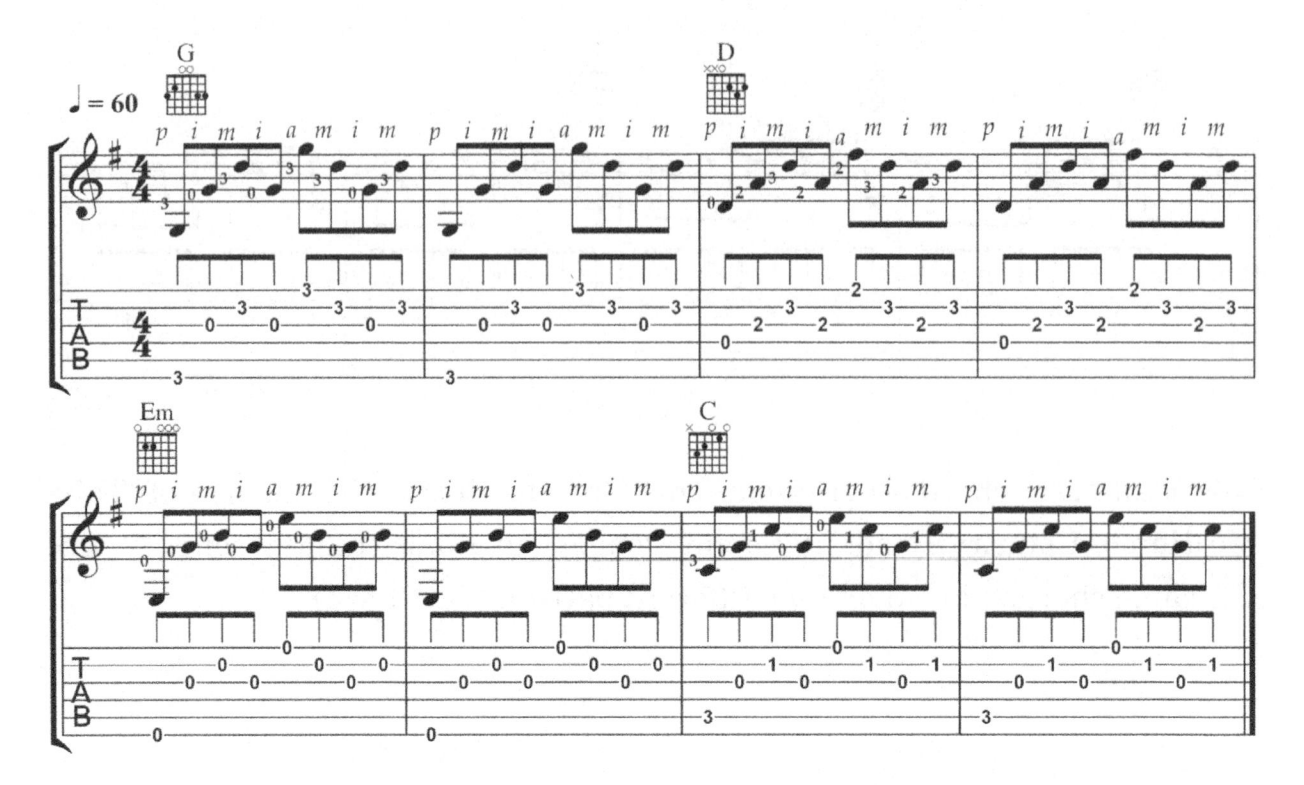

The following chord progression is from "You Are My Sunshine", popularized by Johnny Cash's recording of 1969 but actually written by Jimmie Davis and Charles Mitchell in the 40s.

Pay attention to the C7 chord on the second bar, the fingering on the left hand is like a C chord but adding the pinky on the 3rd fret of string 3. On the third bar, you have an F chord, a barre chord. You'll need to make it right if you want the arpeggios to sound well. Don't despair if you can't pull it off yet, it'll become easier with practice (Ex 5 & 6).

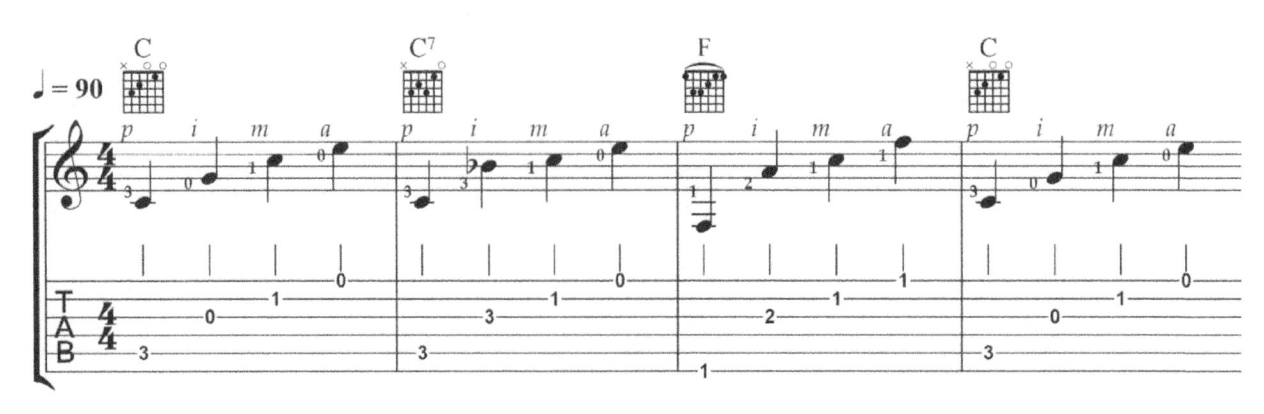

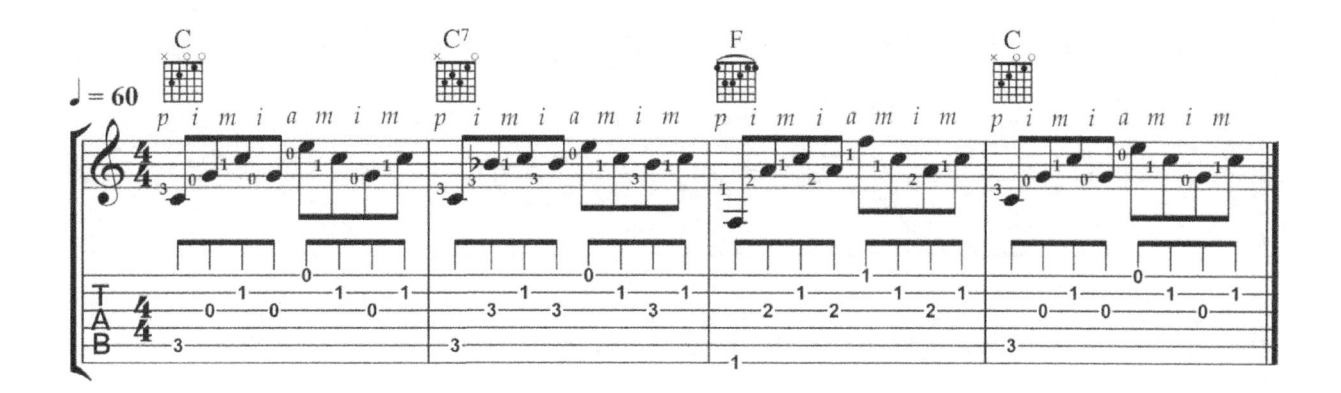

You're approaching a big milestone in the life of every fingerpicking guitar player: playing "Dust in the Wind" by Kansas. I say approaching because we're not quite there yet, but these two exercises are pretty similar to the original song. Don't worry about those scary-looking chord names - it's just normal C and Am chords but changing one single note. Add the pinky or take out the index of your left hand to finger them correctly (Ex 7 & 8).

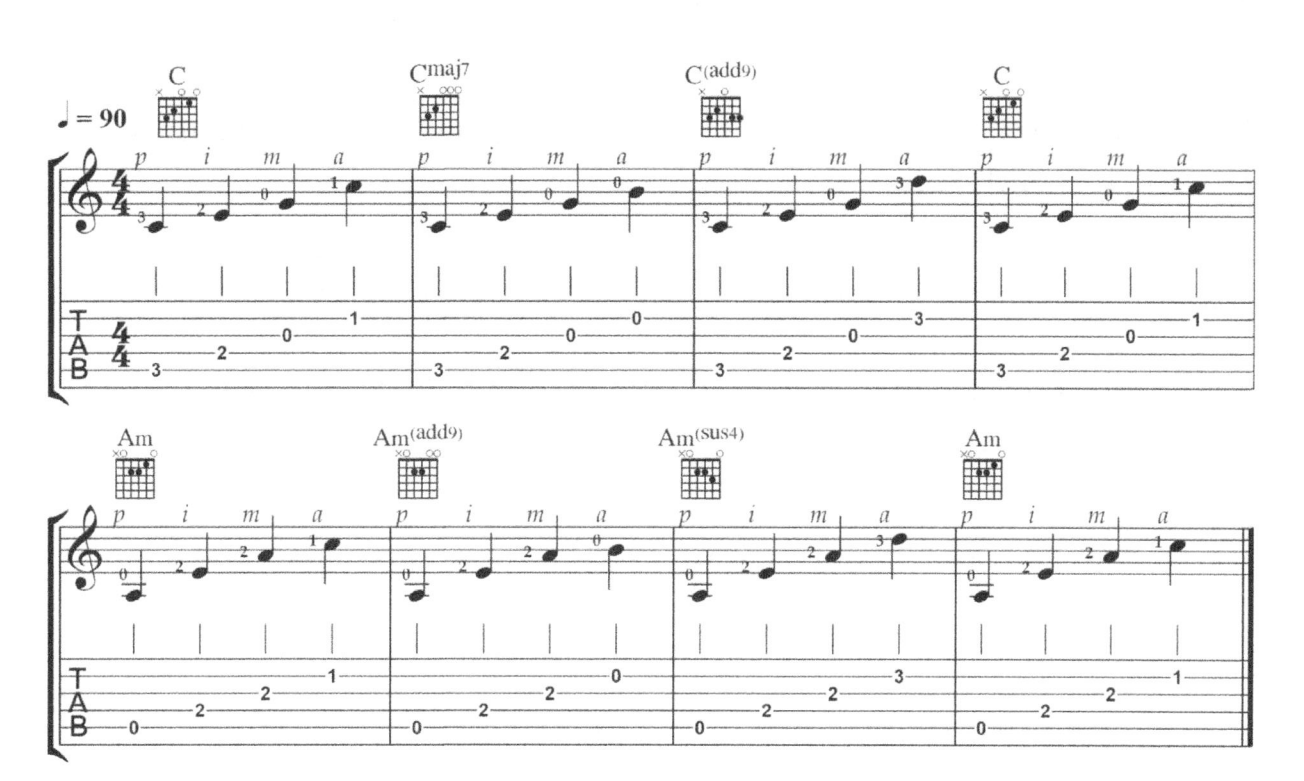

Fingerstyle guitar

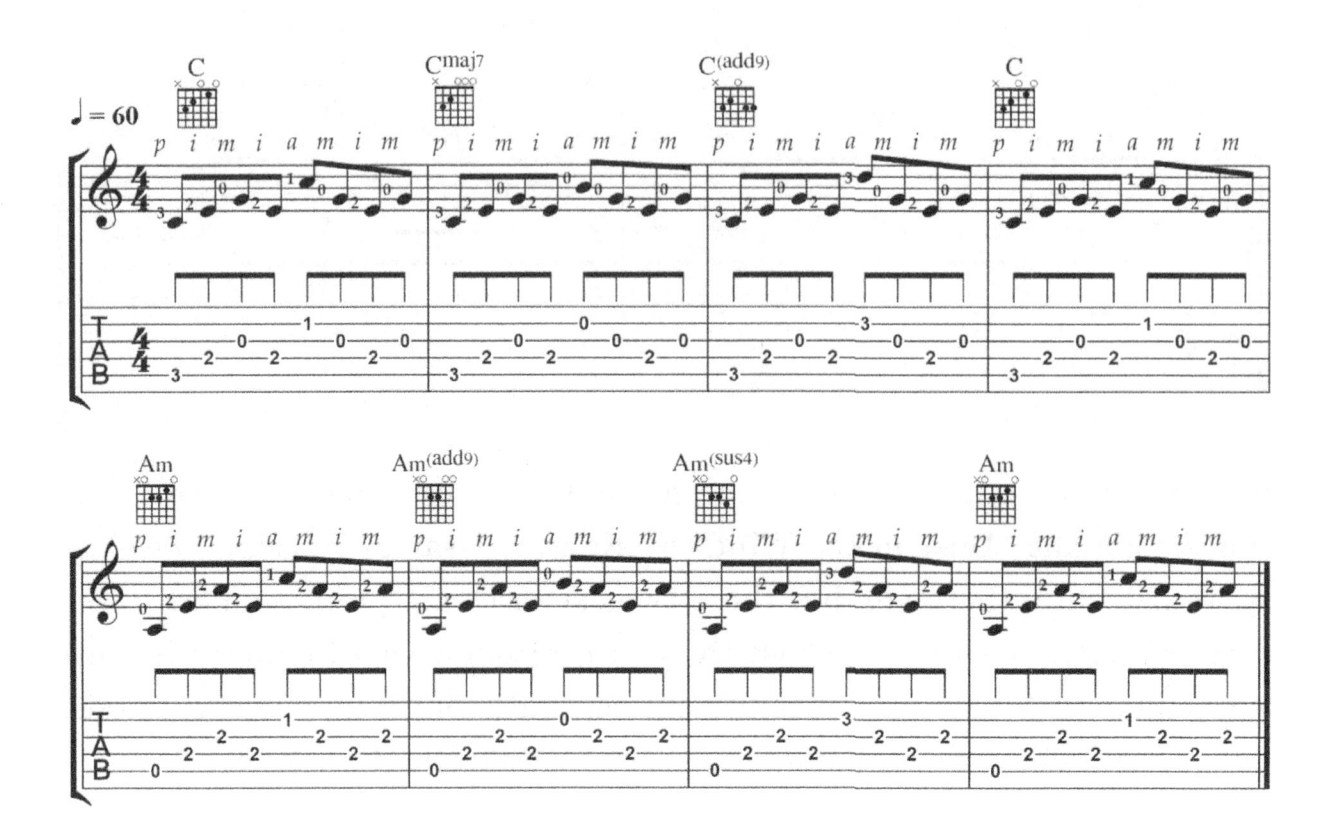

What about trying a blues? And an arpeggiated one! On the second version, try to play it with swing (Ex 9).

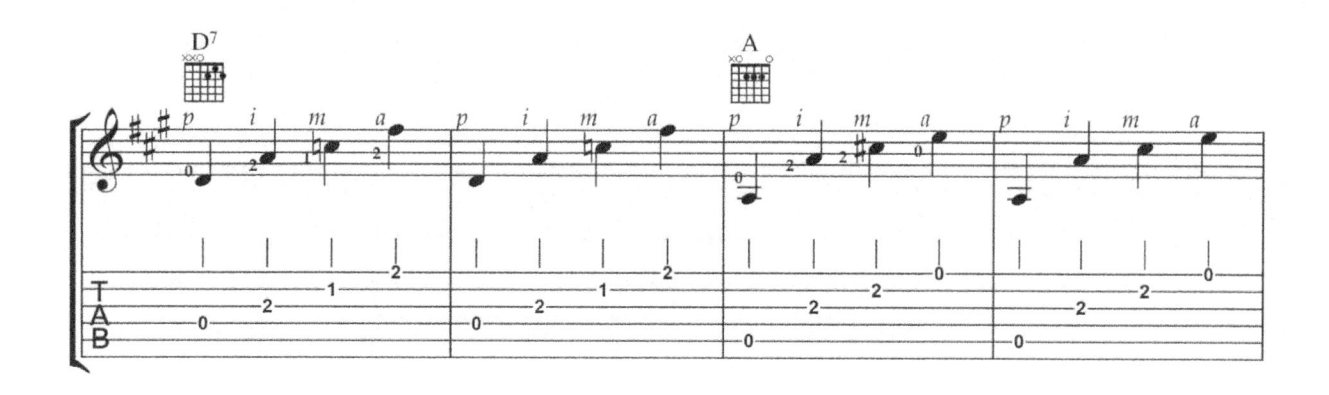

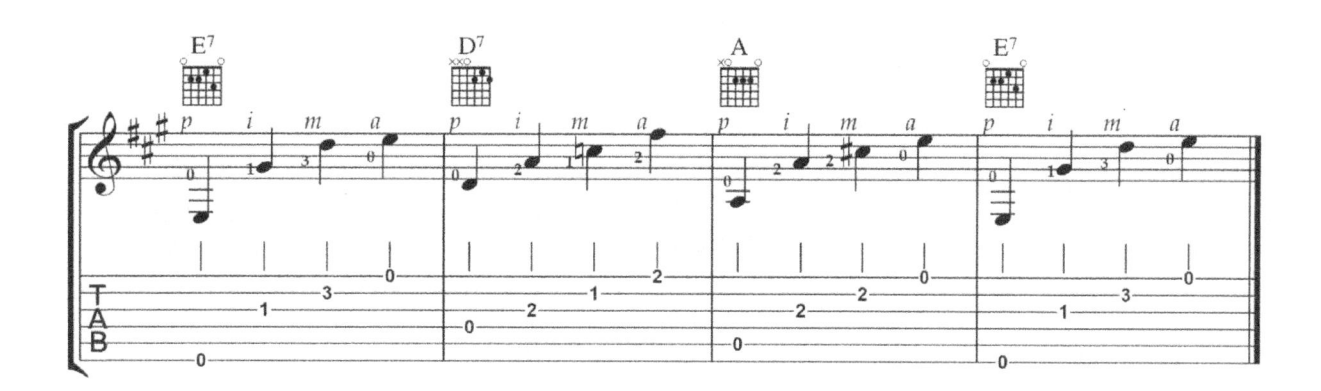

(Ex 10)

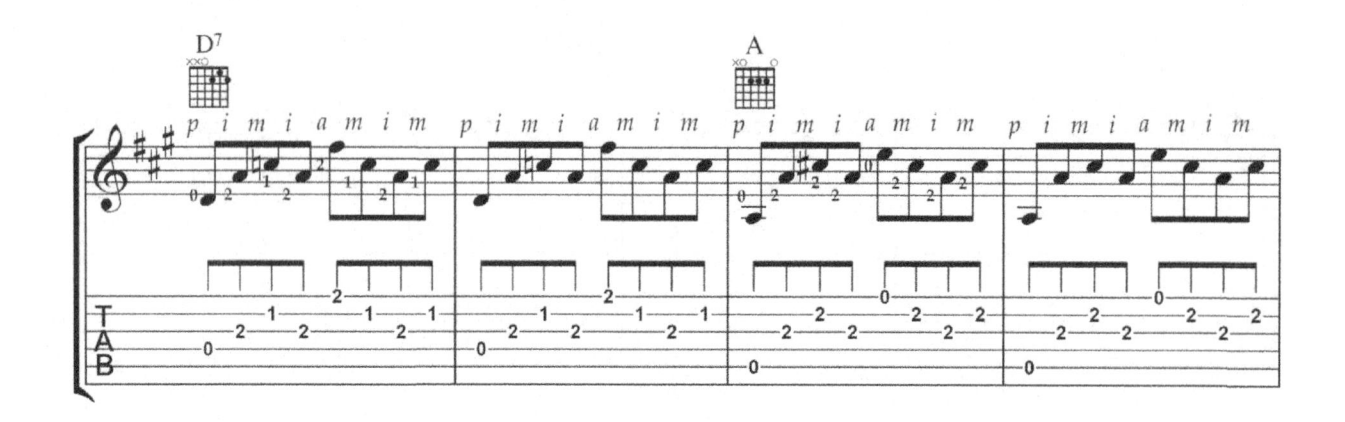

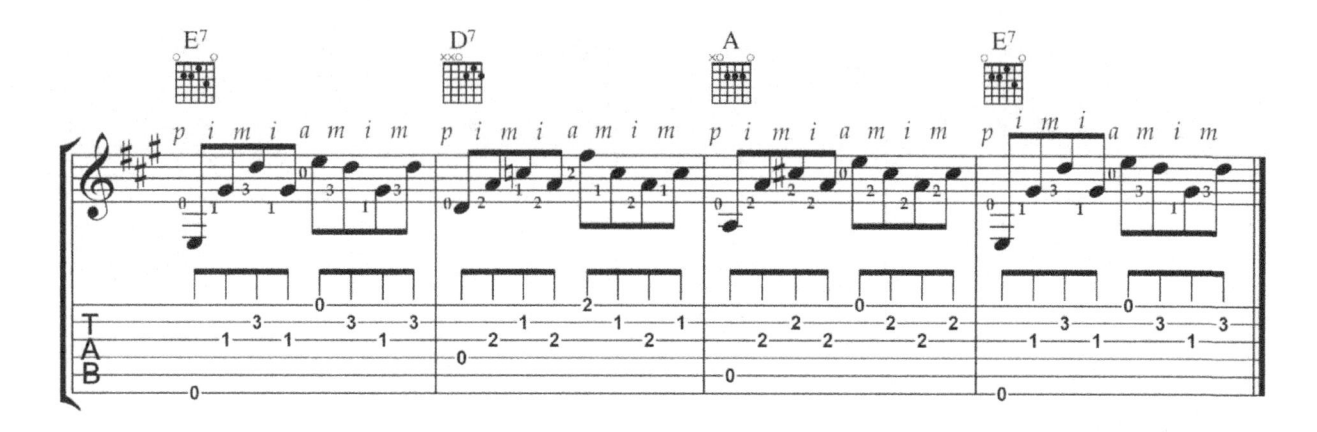

Here's one extra chord progression to finish the level. This one is longer than all the previous ones! (Ex 11 & 12)

Getting Ready For The Real World

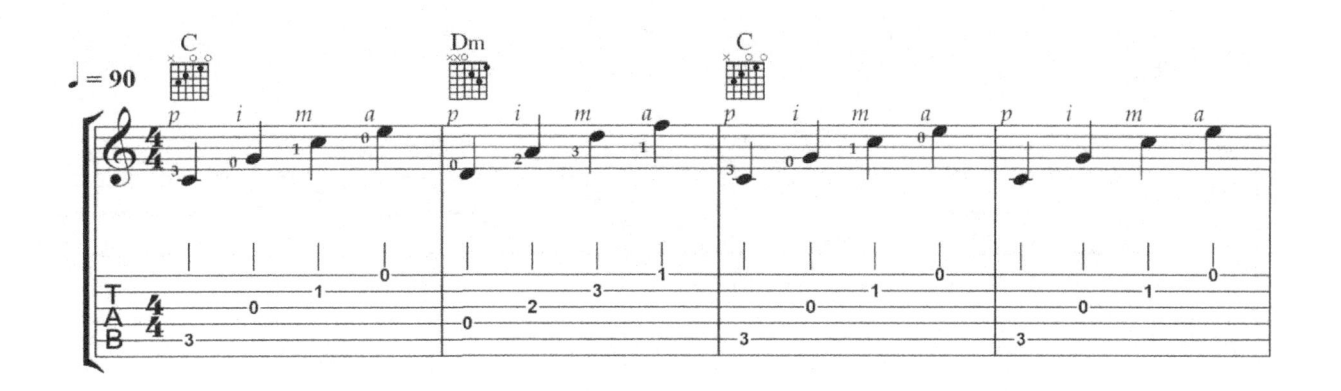

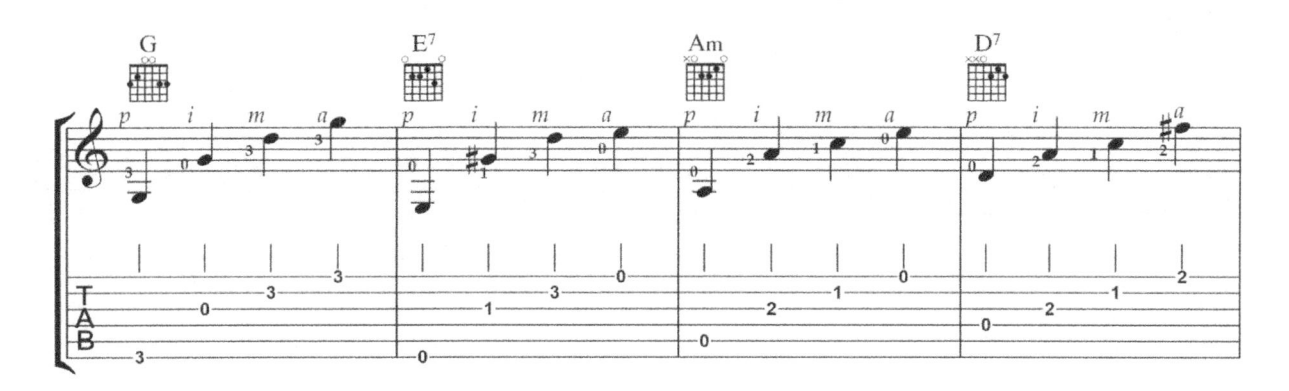

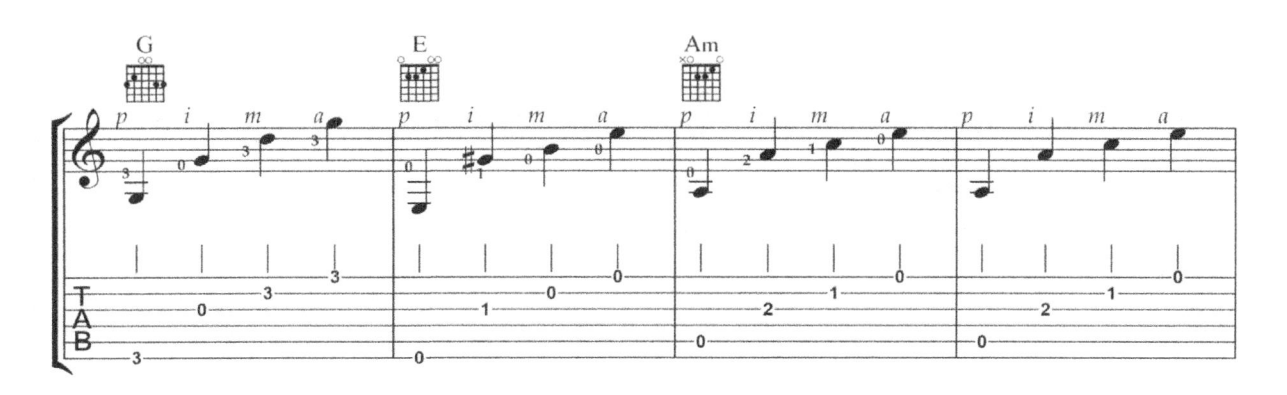

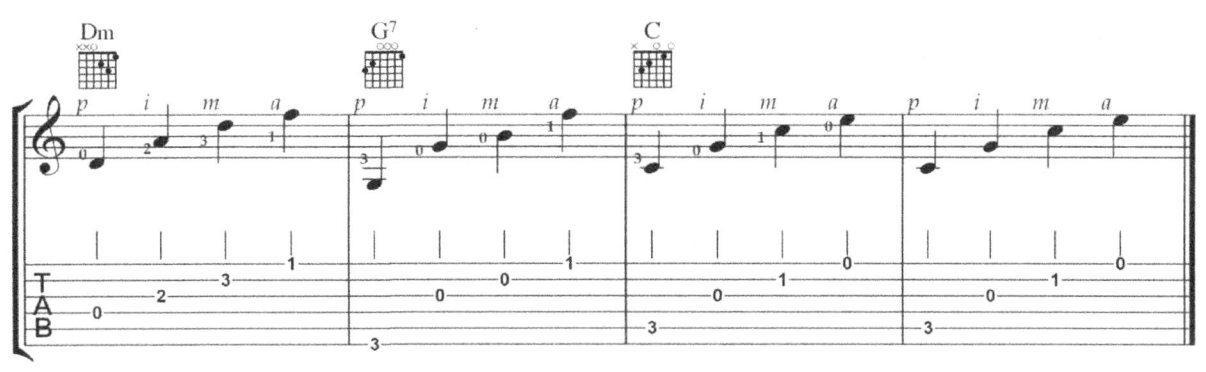

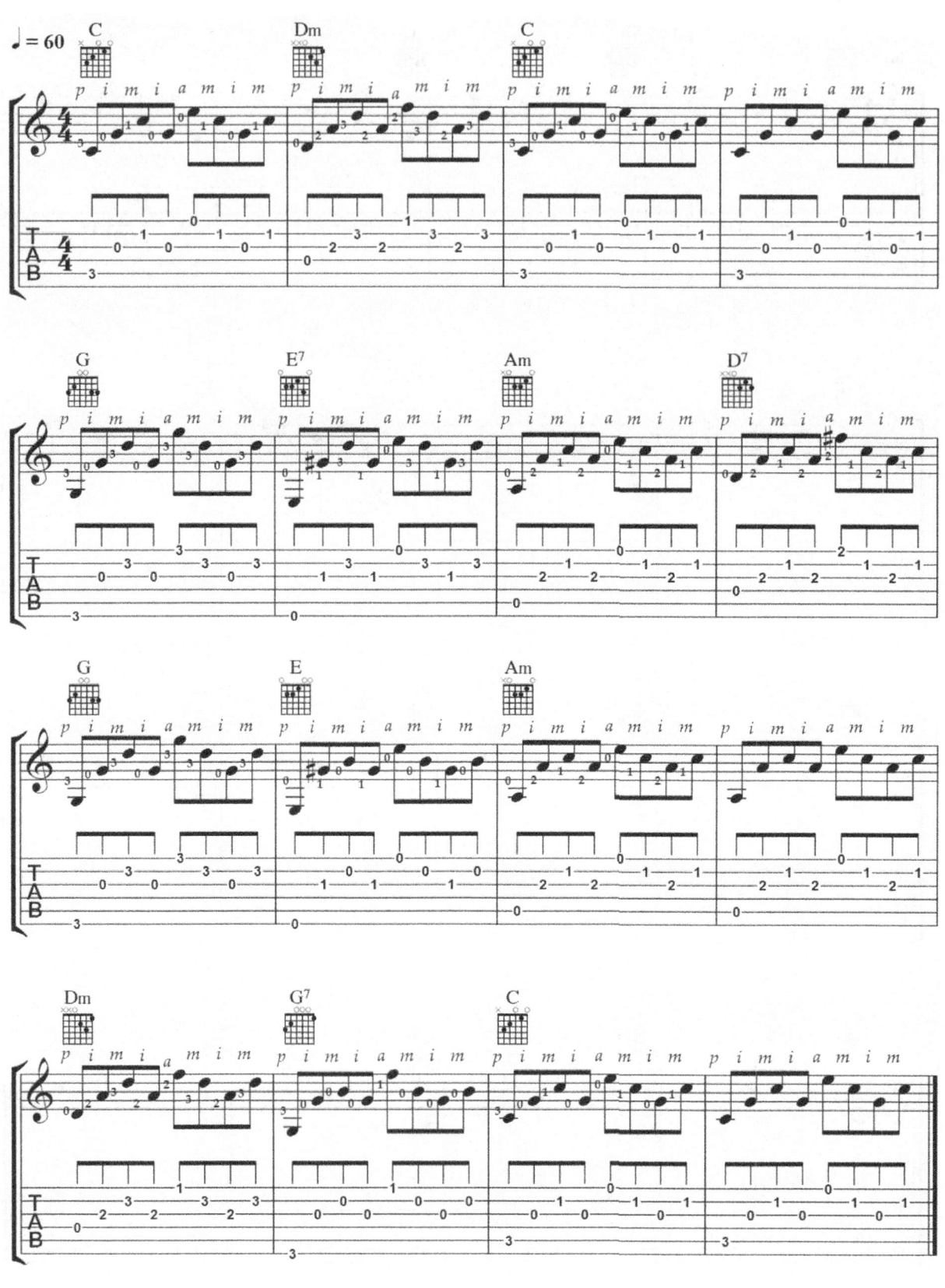

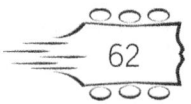

Fingerstyle guitar

Conclusion

You've completed level 5, congratulations! You've played arpeggios on the chords of iconic popular songs. You can already proudly say that you're a capable fingerstyle guitar player now. But don't leave yet - there's a lot more to learn! Jump to the next level to learn more techniques and become even better. If you feel overwhelmed, slow down: perfection doesn't matter, what matters is to keep practicing, to learn a tiny bit every day, and to enjoy the path.

Level 5

~ 4 days ~

You're A Bass Player Now

This time I have bad news for you: you're about to become a bass player. I'm sorry. But every calamity has its bright side - by the end of this level you'll be able to play basslines and chords *at the same time* with your guitar.

Playing bass and chords at the same time is one of the most interesting things you can achieve with fingerpicking guitar, and it can make even the most simple chord progression way more interesting. It sounds a bit as if you were two people playing together, and it can be an impressive sight when done properly.

Most of the time, the thumb will be responsible for playing the bass notes while the other fingers take care of the chords (and eventually melodies, we'll get to that later).

Palm muting the bass

Generally speaking, you can play the bass in two different ways: palm muted or unmuted. Palm muting the bass gives it a more subdued and percussive sound, which often works better as a background layer to let the chords and melodies get the attention they deserve. This is used by many country/folk fingerpicking guitar players, with Chet Atkins and Merle Travis being the two most prominent examples.

To palm mute those bass notes, lightly rest your right hand wrist on the guitar bridge, but make sure it only touches the lower strings playing the bass notes - often strings 6 and 5, sometimes also string 4. The trick is to mute only those few strings while not muting the higher strings so that the latter can ring freely. It takes some practice, so don't despair if it's hard at first. It will get better with practice.

In this level, we're going to practice combining basslines and chords. Let's start with the thumb only. Try to play this part first without palm mute, letting all the notes ring, and then with palm mute. Pay attention to how it changes the sound of your guitar (Ex 1).

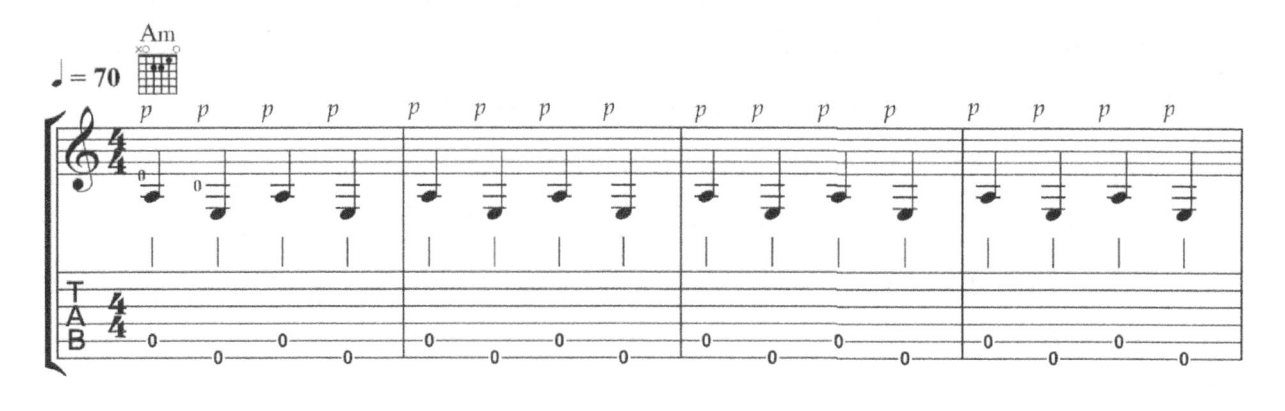

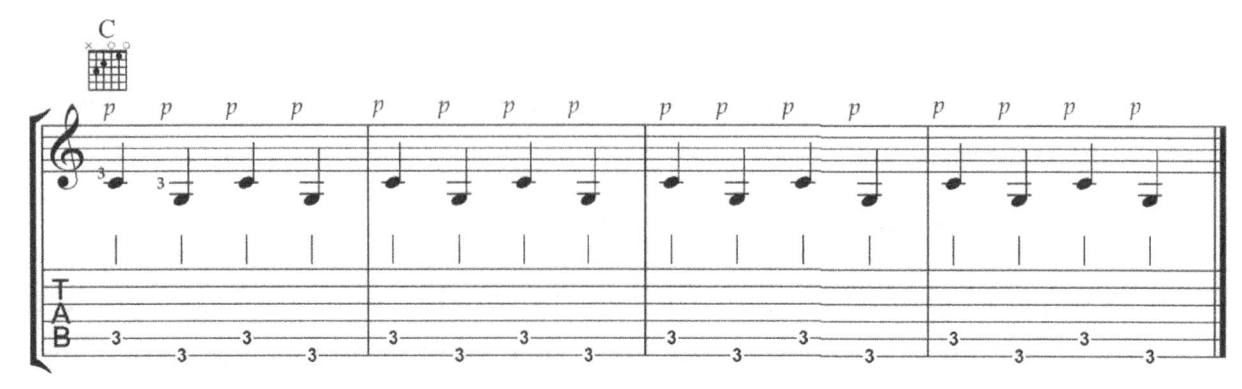

And now let's add chords on top of the same bassline. With your left hand, finger an Am during the first half and a C during the second half. The rest is up to your right hand. As in the previous exercise, try to play it first without palm muting and then with palm muting. Try to mute only the strings with the bassline (strings 5 and 6) while letting all the other strings ring. For the bassline during the C chord, your left hand ring finger will have to be jumping between the 3rd frets of strings 5 and 6 (Ex 2).

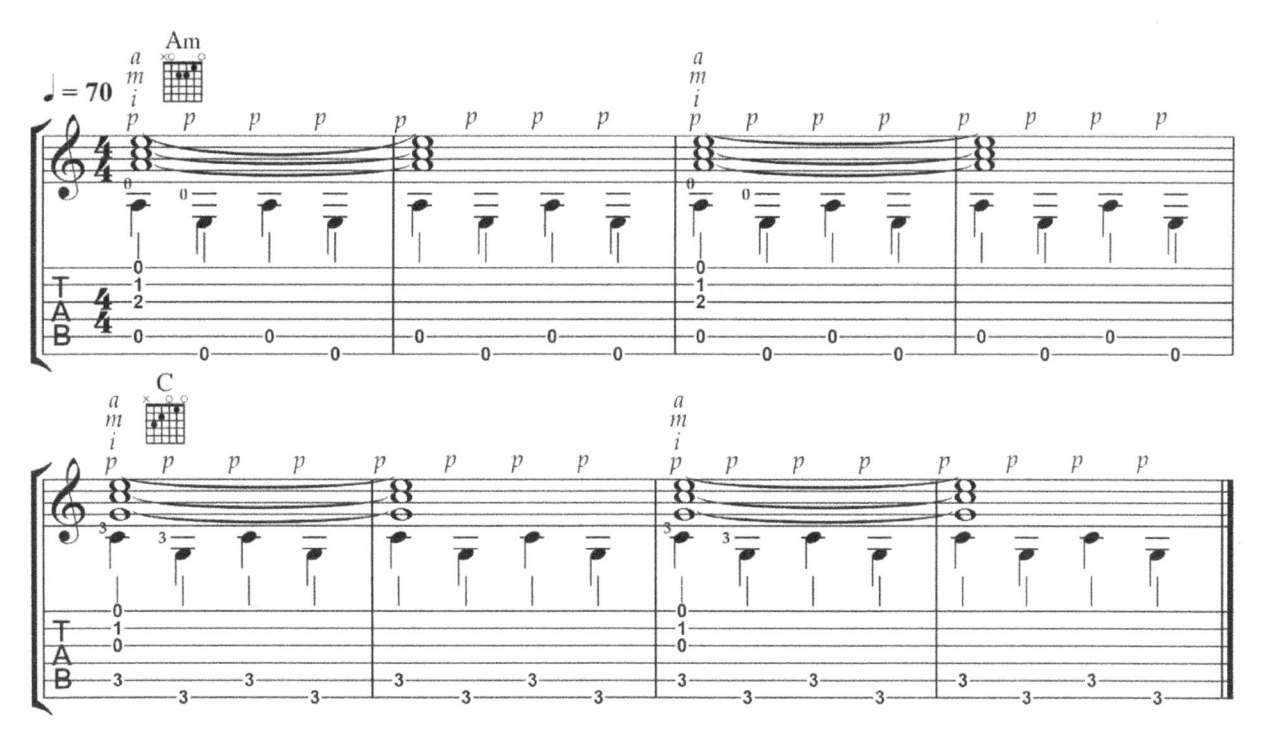

This is a similar chord progression but in another key, with chords Em and G. As in the previous progression, let's start with the bass only. Notice how on the G chord your thumb has to jump from string 6 to string 4, skipping string 5 (Ex 3).

> **Note** : Audio tracks for these exercises are available in bonus section at the start of the book.

Fingerstyle guitar

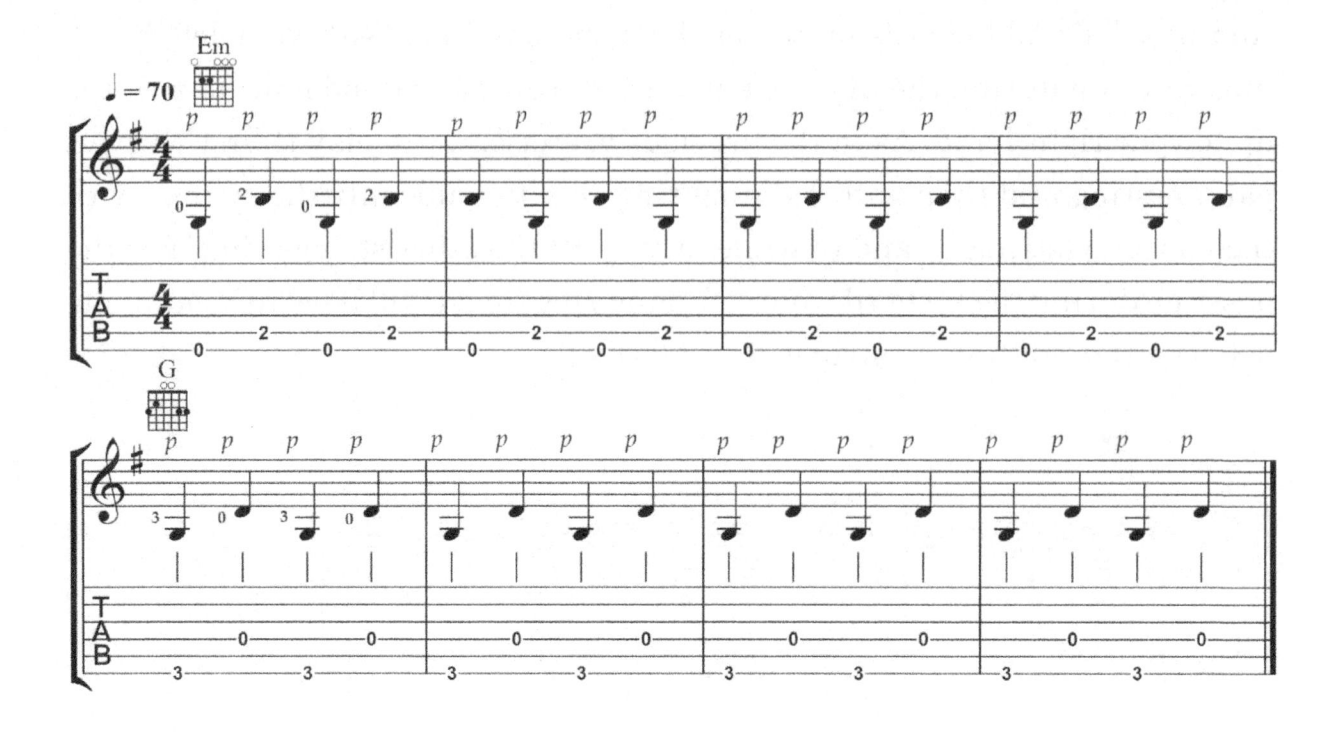

And now with chords (Ex 4).

Let's try one more exercise like this (Ex 5 & 6).

Now we're going to add rhythm to those chords. Let's start with bass-only again (Ex 7).

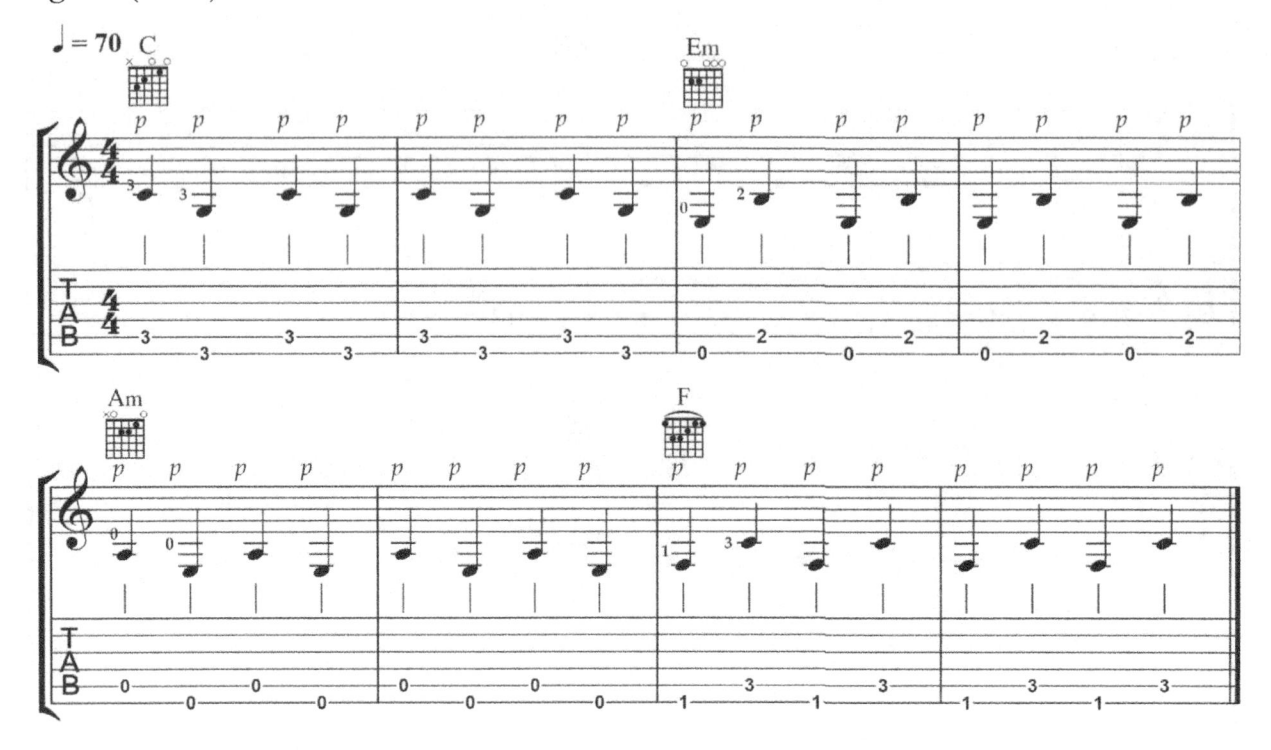

This rhythm is a common syncopated rhythm that works well with a lot of modern music. Start easy, it can be confusing to read the notation at first. When playing it pay attention to that tricky F barre chord (Ex 8).

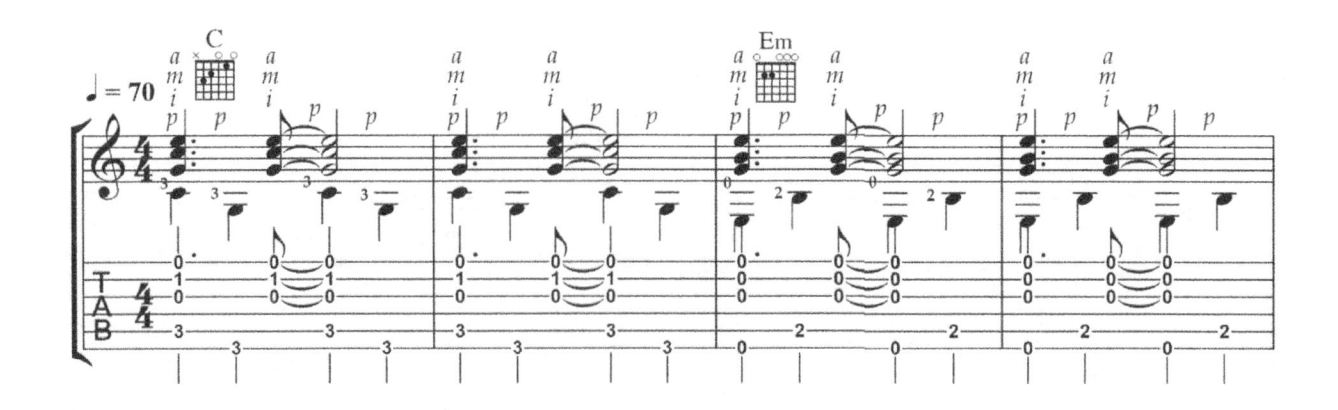

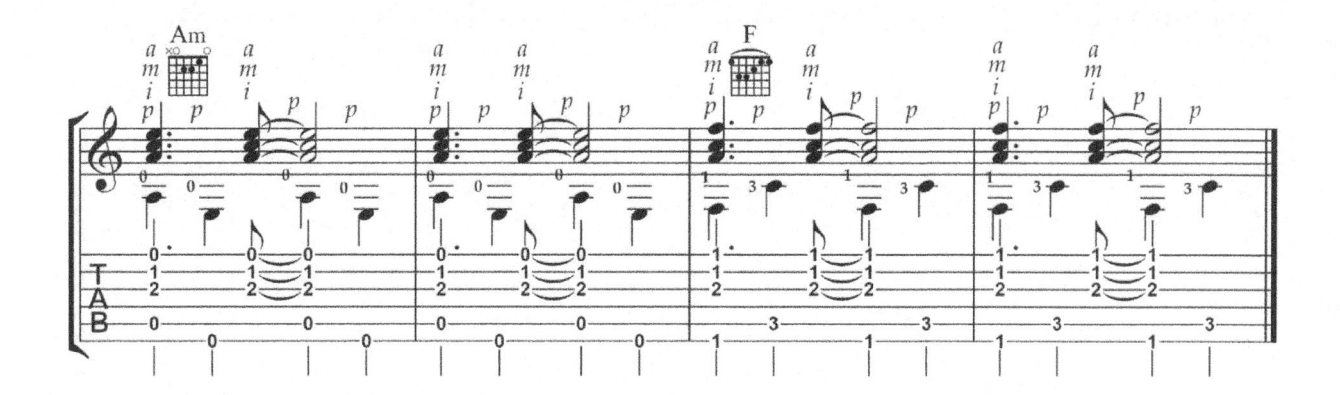

Walking bass

Well done! The basslines you've just played can bring life to any chord progression. What we played are relatively simple bass patterns, which are already an achievement since we're playing bass and chords at the same time. But basslines can go even further.

I'm going to show you some walking basslines - basslines that "walk" around as if they had a life on their own, similar to the basslines played in Jazz music.

Let's start with the first one, again with only bass. Later we'll add chords on top of it. Try to already play it while fingering the specified chords, even if you're still not playing them. You'll see how you'll sometimes have to lift some of your left hand fingers from their chord position in order to fret all the notes, as in the last note of the 3rd bar. Use the left hand index finger on that note on the 1st fret (Ex 9).

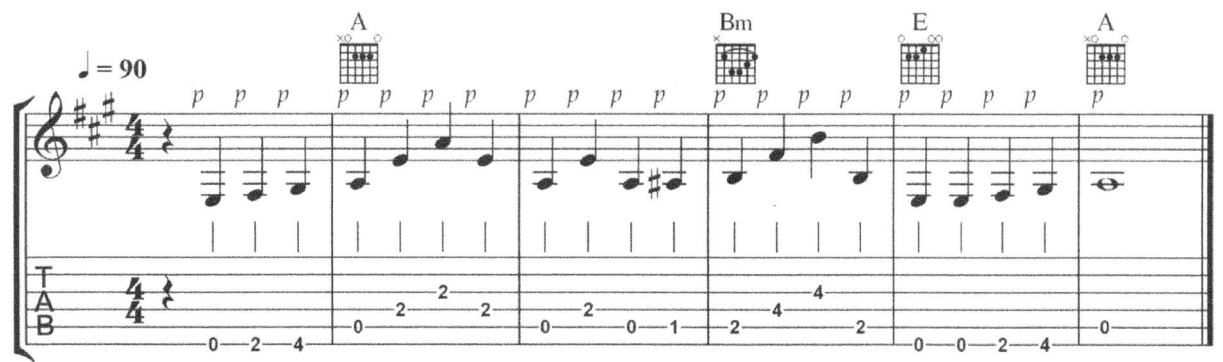

Now with chords on top of the same walking bass (Ex 10).

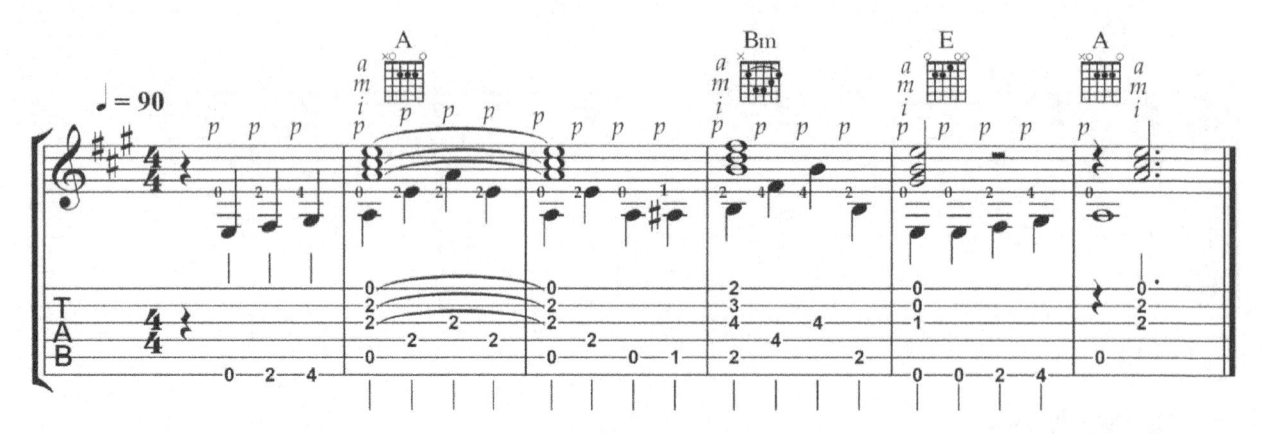

In the first bar of the next exercise, either use your pinky to finger the last note on the 4th fret, or use the ring finger (you'll have to momentarily stop fingering the chord for that). On the second bar, release the left hand index from the chord to play the 1st and 2nd frets. These situations where we have to sacrifice part of the chord notes to be able to play the bass are normal when it comes to complex basslines like this one. This is a limitation of the guitar that we have to get used to (Ex 11).

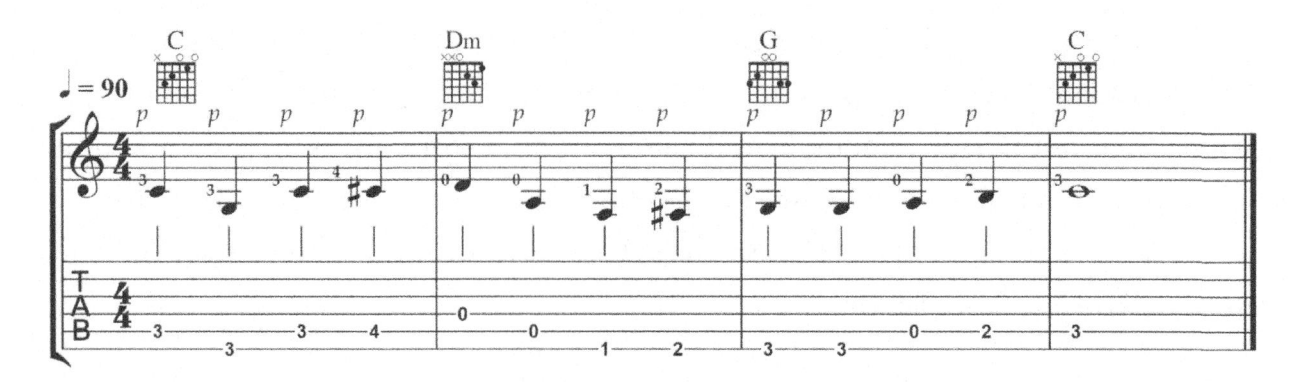

And now, with chords (Ex 12).

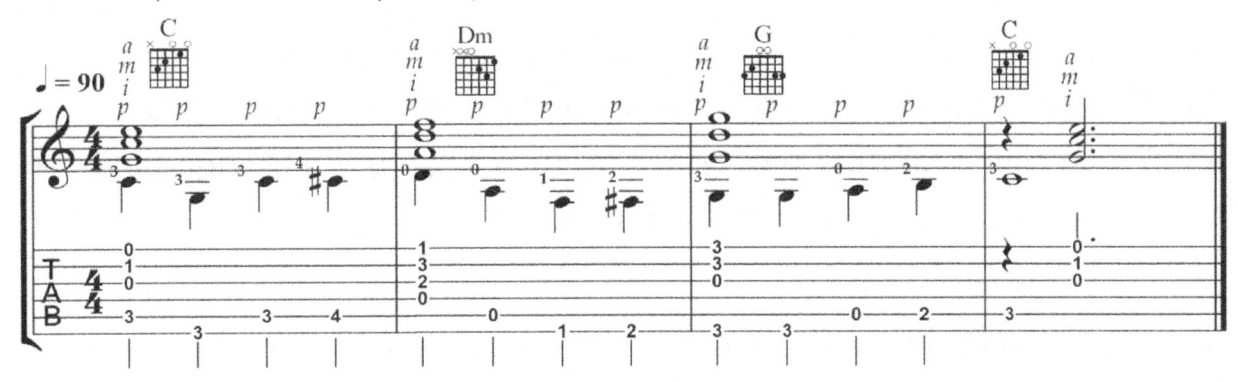

Now we're going to try something different - instead of adding chords on top of a bassline, we're going to add higher notes to fill the gaps between bass notes. This creates a somewhat classical sound, especially if you don't use palm mute on the bass notes. Try to play this one with and without palm mute on the lower strings to see the difference.

We start with bass only and then we'll add the notes in between (Ex 13 & 14).

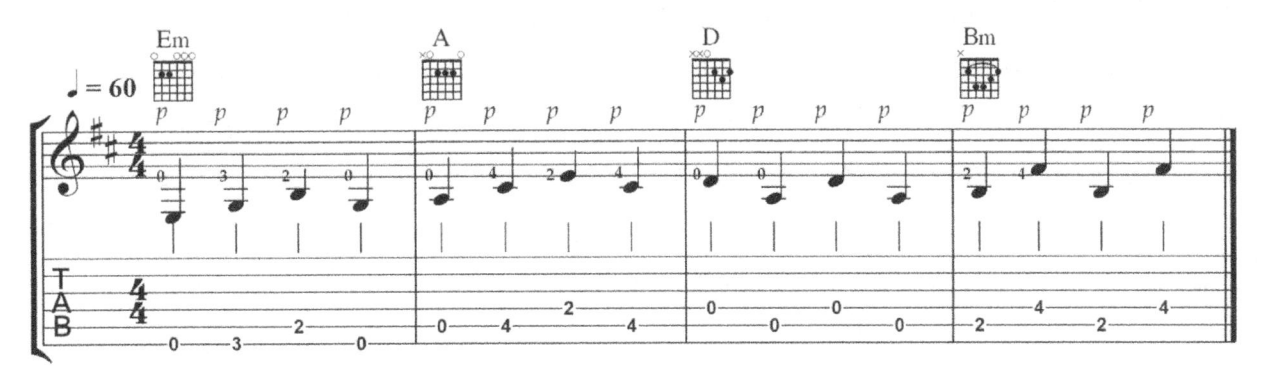

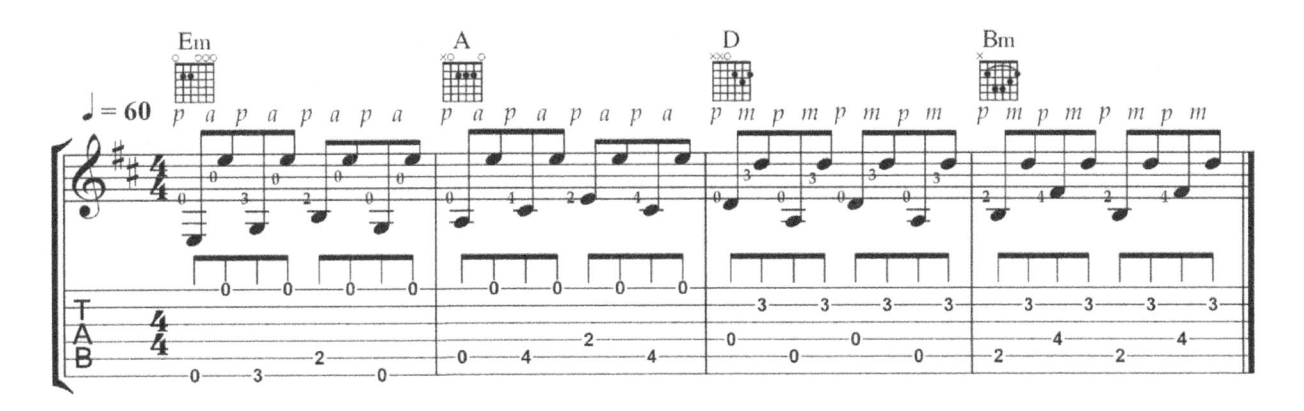

Muting the bass notes

Muting the bass strings is not the same as palm muting them. Palm muting means using your right hand wrist to partly mute the strings and achieve a different sound. Muting the strings means using your left hand fingers to completely stop the string from ringing, in order to stop the note.

Muting bass notes is useful to make the bassline clearer whenever you're not using palm mute - the idea is to only have only one single bass line sounding at all times, without overlapping bass notes. While overlapping bass notes aren't catastrophic, having only one bass note sounding will improve your performance.

Muting bass notes is especially useful when playing without palm muting the lower strings. Palm muting the low strings already shortens its sound so it's not that critical to mute the bass notes.

When the bass note is a fretted one, simply release pressure on that left hand finger to stop the note. But the tricky part comes with open strings, since they're not fretted. You can mute an open string by using one of your free fingers on your left hand, if any. However, that's not always possible, as fingerpikcing guitar often keeps all your fingers busy. A trick to overcome this is to use your left hand thumb (yes, the *left hand* one!). This is a bit of an advanced technique and can feel weird at first, but if you stretch your thumb you might be able to touch strings 6, 5, and even 4, effectively stopping them. Yet you will only be able to stop the lowest sounding bass note this way since you can't stop string 5 without stopping also string 6. So if you've just played string 6, you can stop it at the same time you play string 5, but you cannot do the opposite - it's not possible to stop string 5 with the thumb while playing string 6 at the same time. However, this already can make a big difference in your sound.

Keep in mind that the extent to which you can do this will depend on your hand size, so if you have small hands make sure you don't overstretch them and hurt yourself.

Another one, starting with the bass only again. Stop the bass notes during the stop (Ex 15).

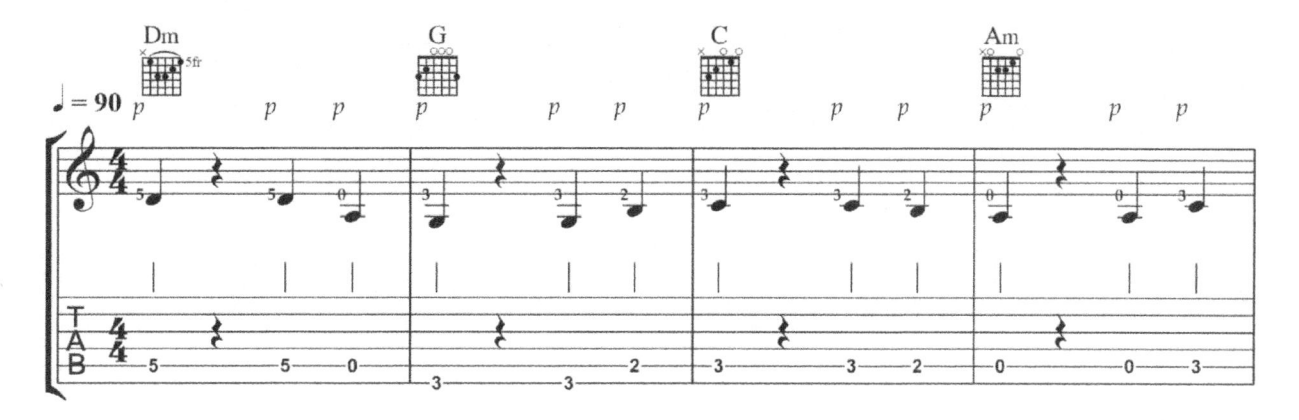

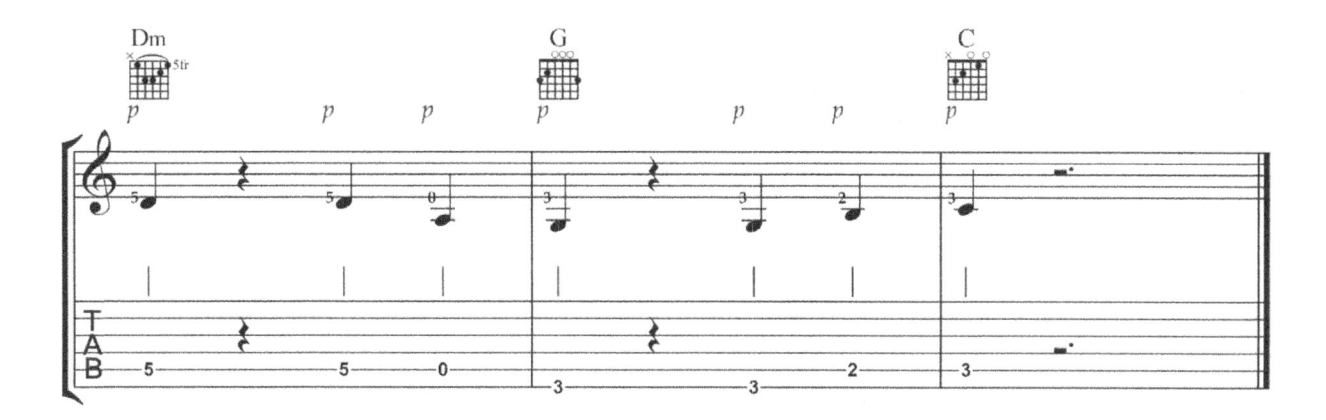

And now, with chords on the second beat of each bar, on strings 1, 2, and 3. Usually it's better to let the high strings ring for a better sonority, but in this case don't let them ring to make it sound more rhythmic (Ex 16).

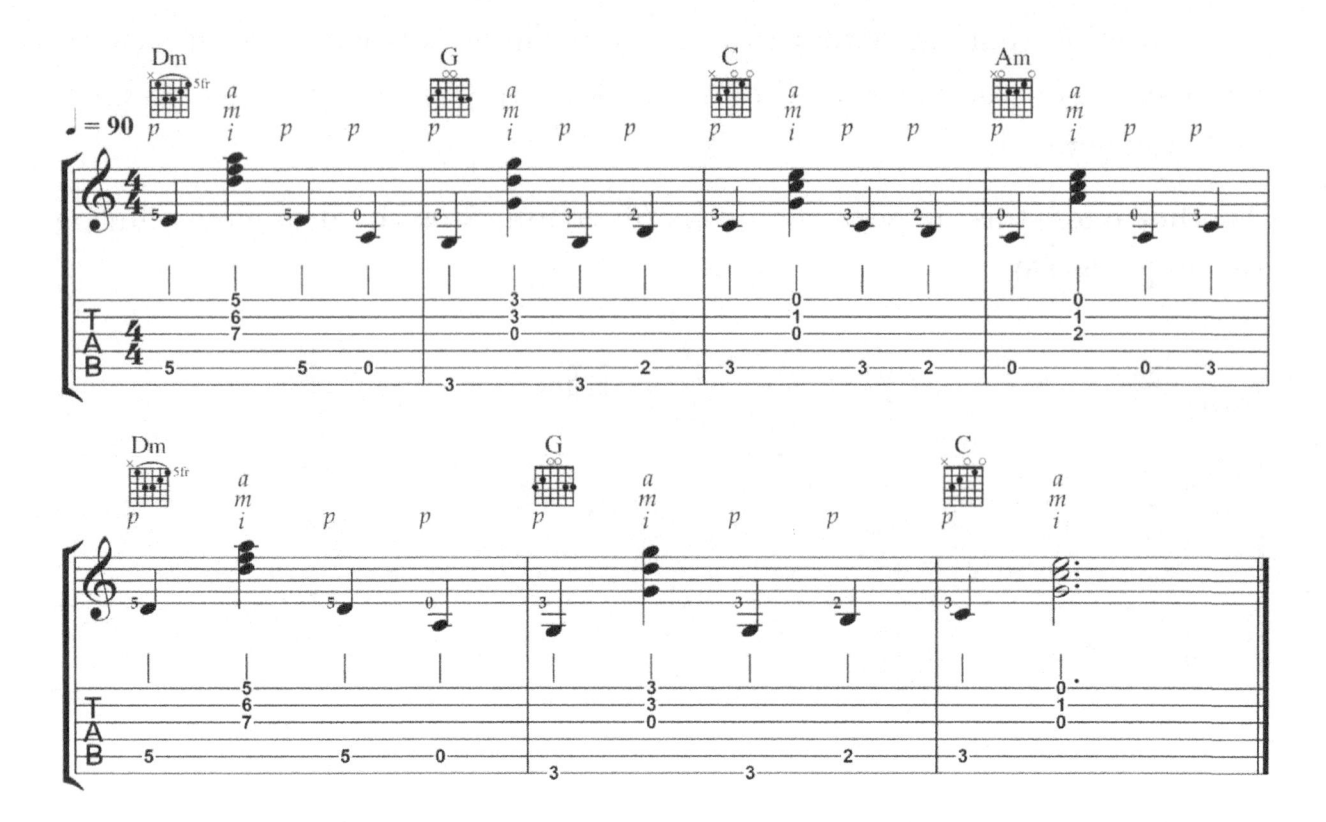

Let's try to mix arpeggio patterns with a walking bass. Let the high notes ring as usual in this one (Ex 17).

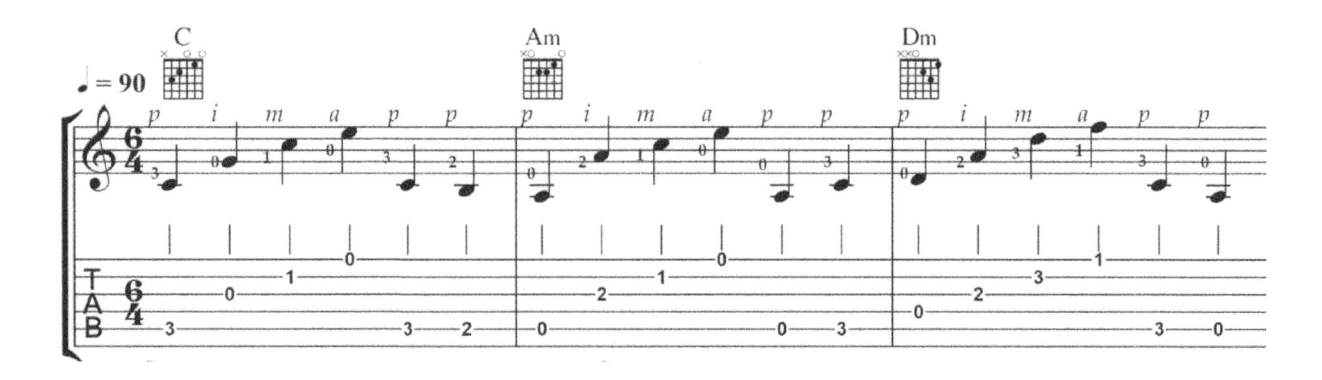

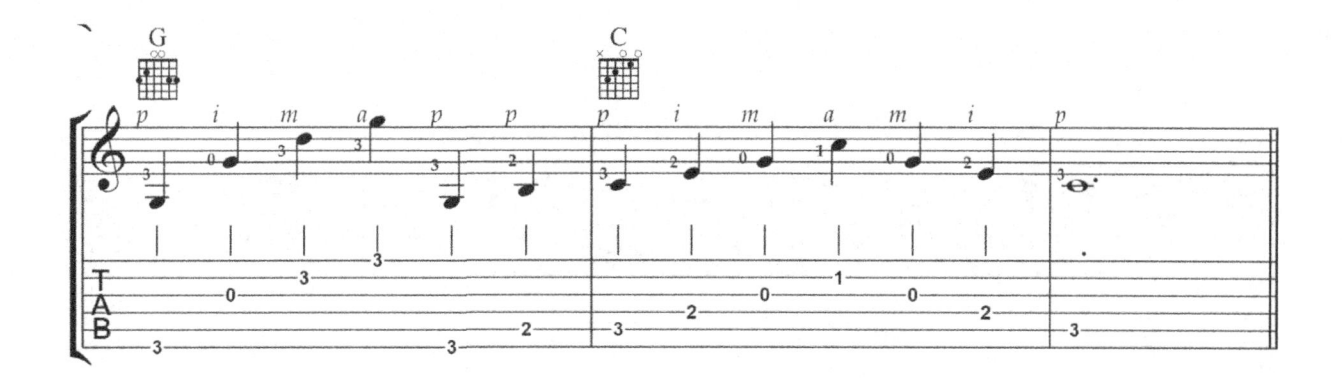

One last one to finish the level: when playing the version with chords, try to play it both letting them ring and without letting them ring, to see how they sound. When you let them ring the part sounds fuller, but when you don't, it has more momentum (Ex 18 & 19).

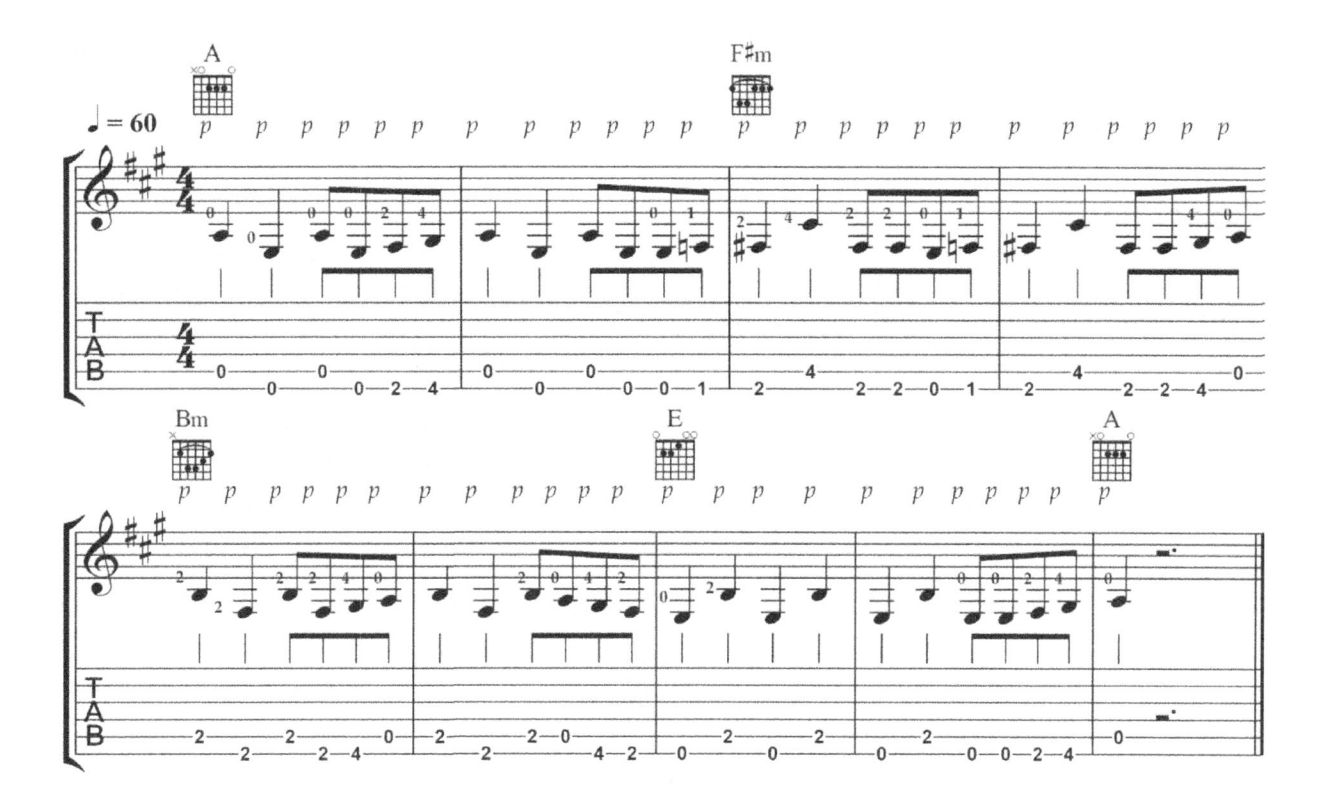

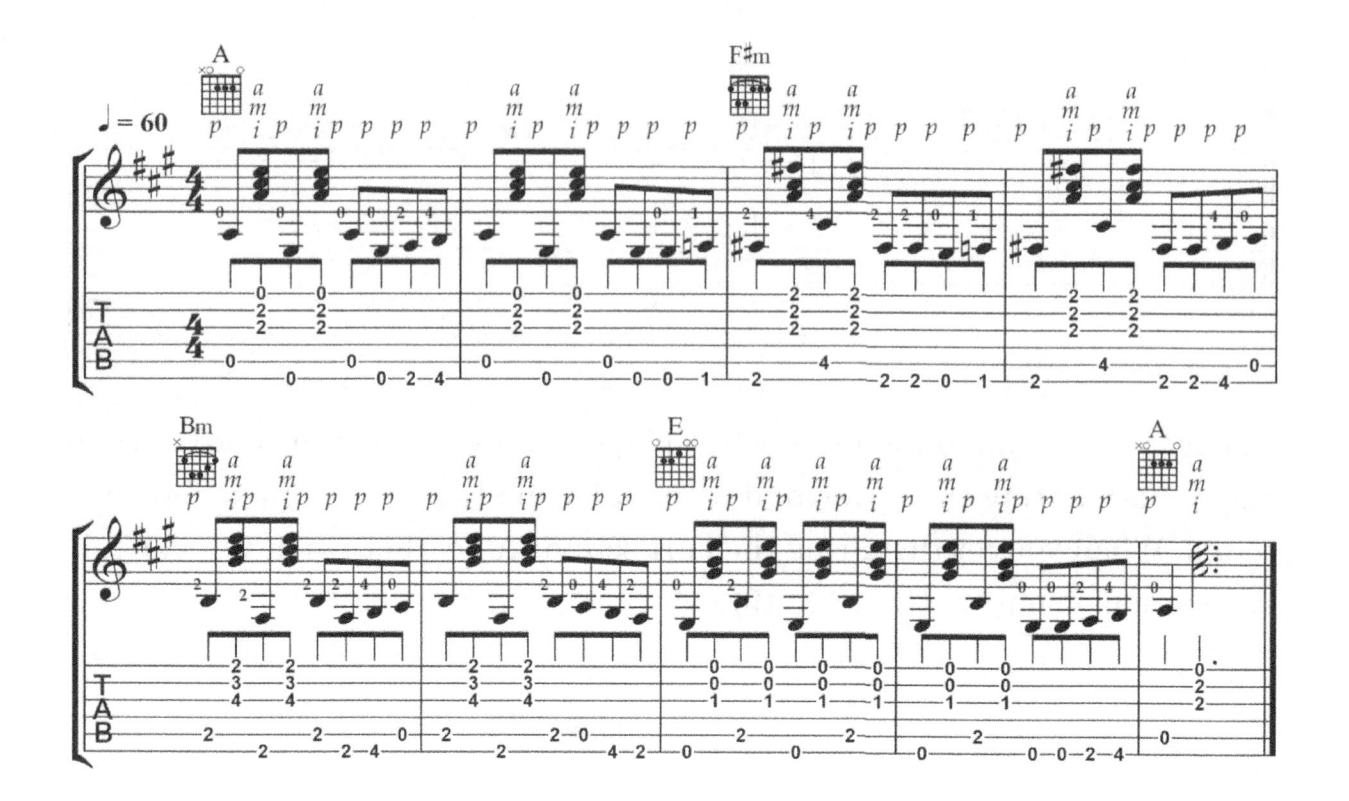

Conclusion

Congratulations on finishing another level. While earlier in the book we took a look at using your right hand fingers and then at arpeggio patterns, now we explored the possibilities of playing basslines with your guitar. You'll never have to play with bass players again since you can do it all yourself!

Now that you've set yourself up for a bassist-free life, let's put it all together and start playing fingerpicking guitar songs - the ones that make others wonder how is it possible to play so many notes on a single guitar.

Level 6

~ 4 days ~

Arranging Simple Songs

Happy Birthday

You're about to become the soul of every birthday party: the first full fingerpicking song you'll learn is said to date from 1893. Originally made as a school greeting song, it later evolved into the most popular birthday song ever.

But let's do it step by step. First, play this version with bass only so that you can practice that before adding the melody on top of it. The fermata in the F chord bar means that you can let ring the note as much as you want (this is the moment where you say the name of the birthday guy!).

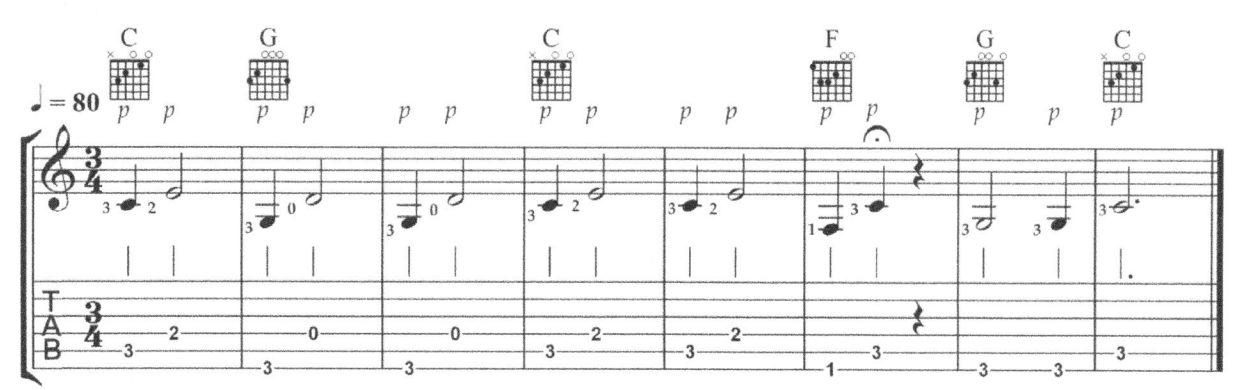

Fingerstyle guitar

This song has a well-known melody that we'll play on top of the bassline - let's practice the melody on its own first. The *pima* notation on the top of each bar will indicate what right hand finger you have to use for each note.

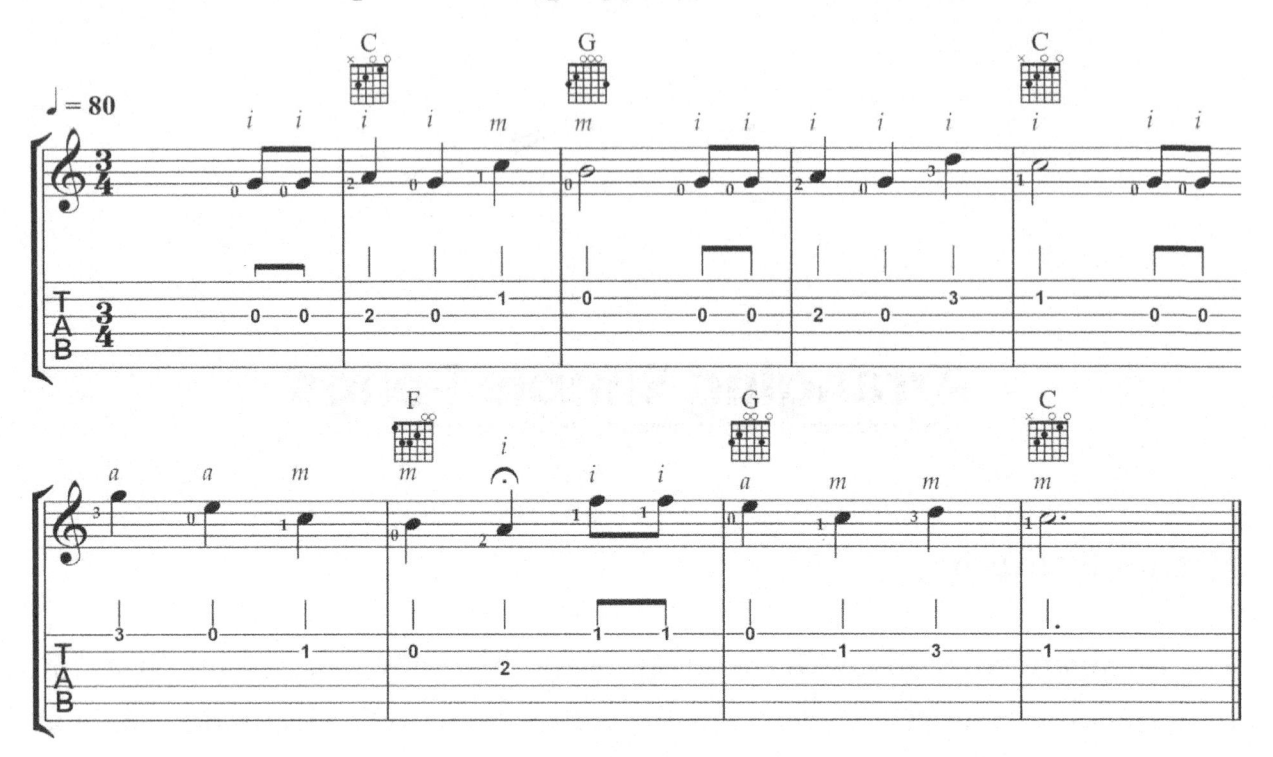

Good. Ready for the whole thing? You'll see that since you'll also be playing the bassline your fingers won't be that free to play the melody. To figure out which left hand fingers to use for each note, first finger the chord written on top of the bar. Then look at which fingers you won't use to play the bass notes. From these, use the one that feels the most comfortable for each melody note.

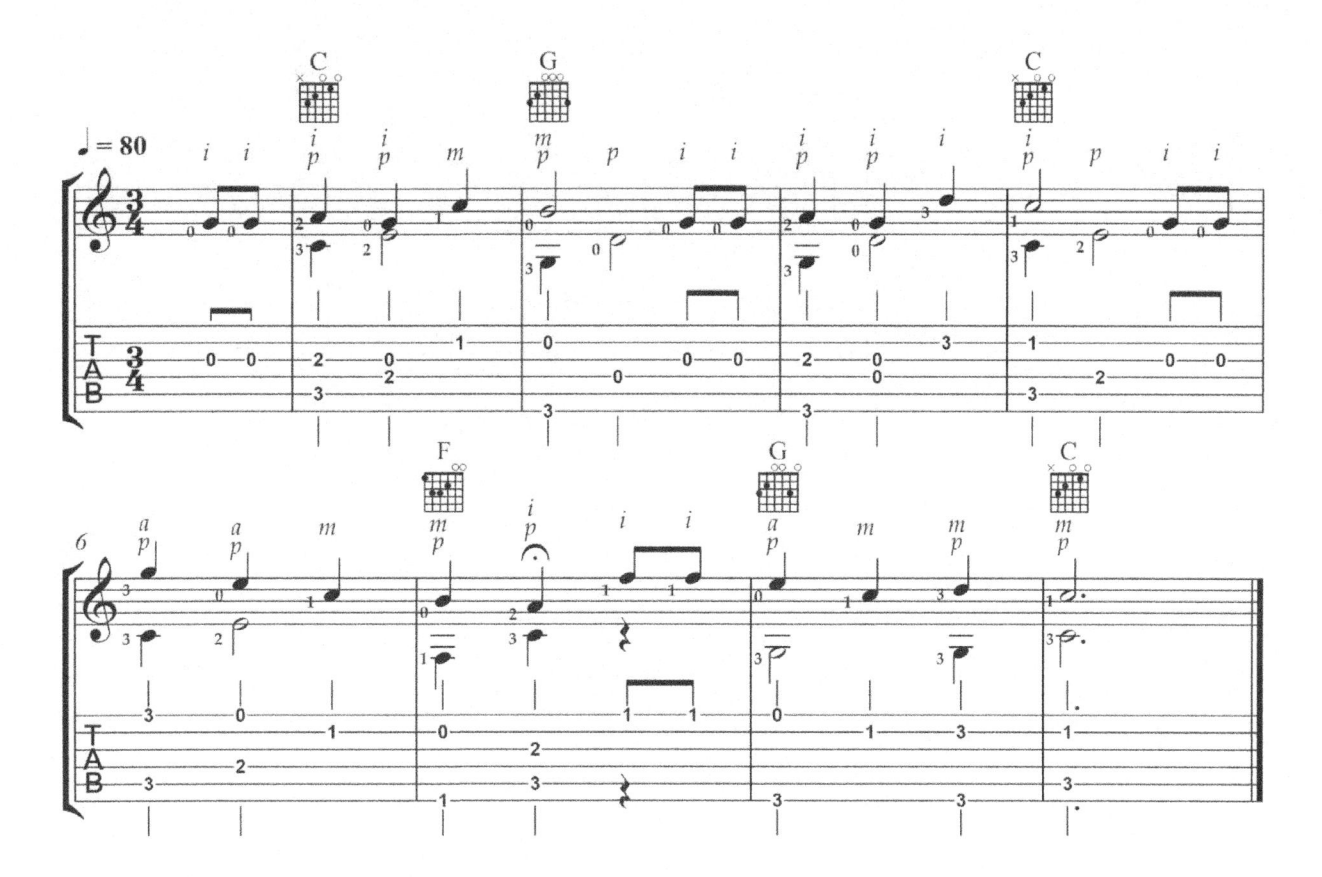

Oh When the Saints Go Marching In

Great job on tackling the birthday song. Let's keep the momentum with another iconic song! "When the Saints Go Marching In" was originally a black spiritual, and it was later recorded and popularized by Louis Amstrong in 1938. And now, you're about to learn it.

Let's start with the bassline again. This is optional, but try to mute string 6 with the thumb every time you play string 5 during the whole song. And if you can reach it, mute string 5 every time you play string 4 during the D chord bar.

Fingerstyle guitar

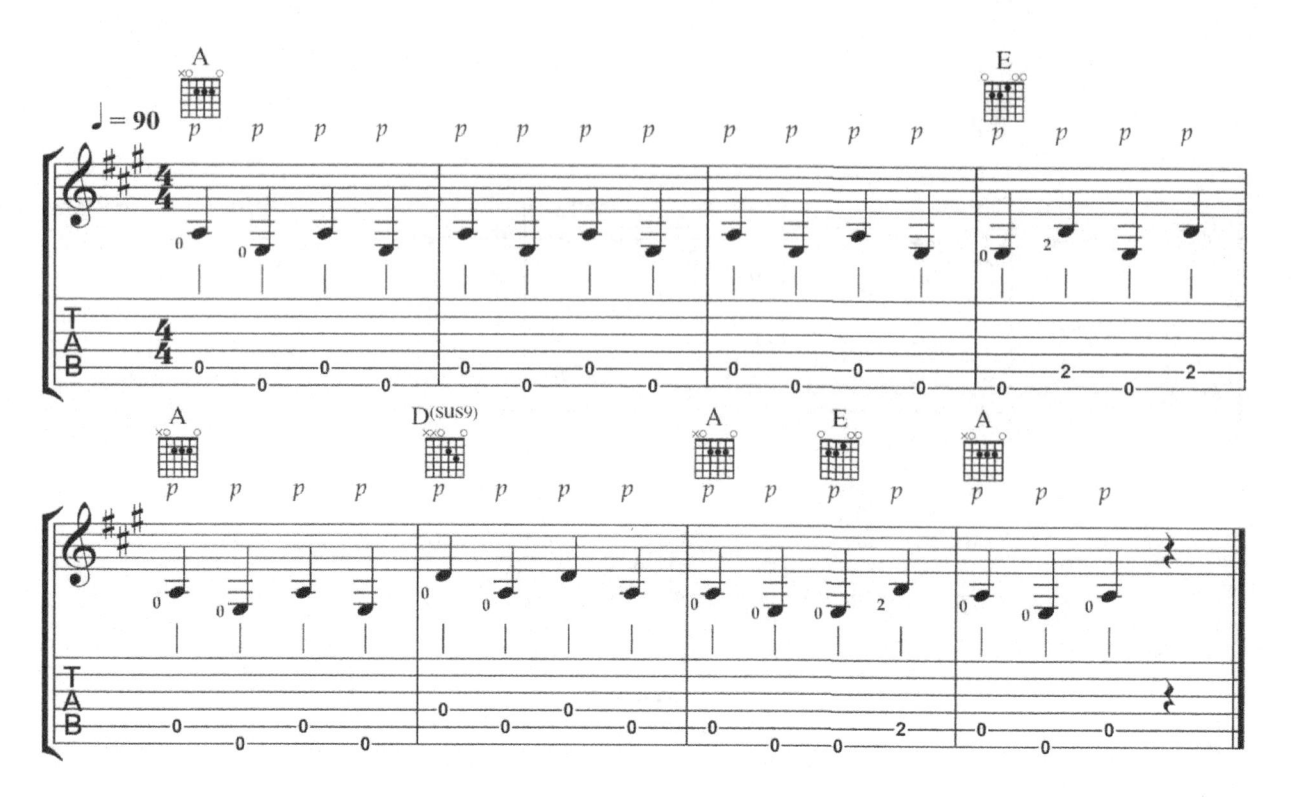

Now let's go for the melody.

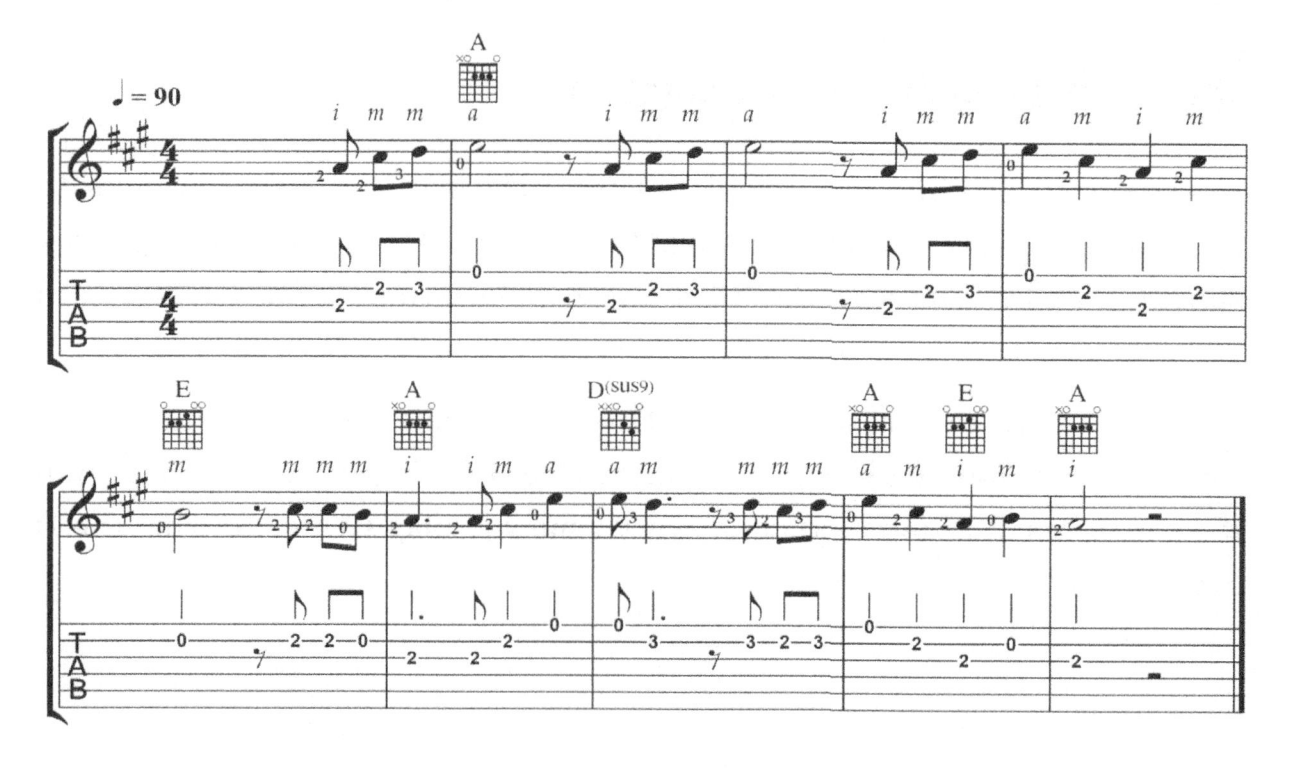

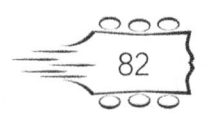

And now the whole thing. It's a lot of notes to keep an eye on, so start practicing it very, very slow. Use a metronome if you can.

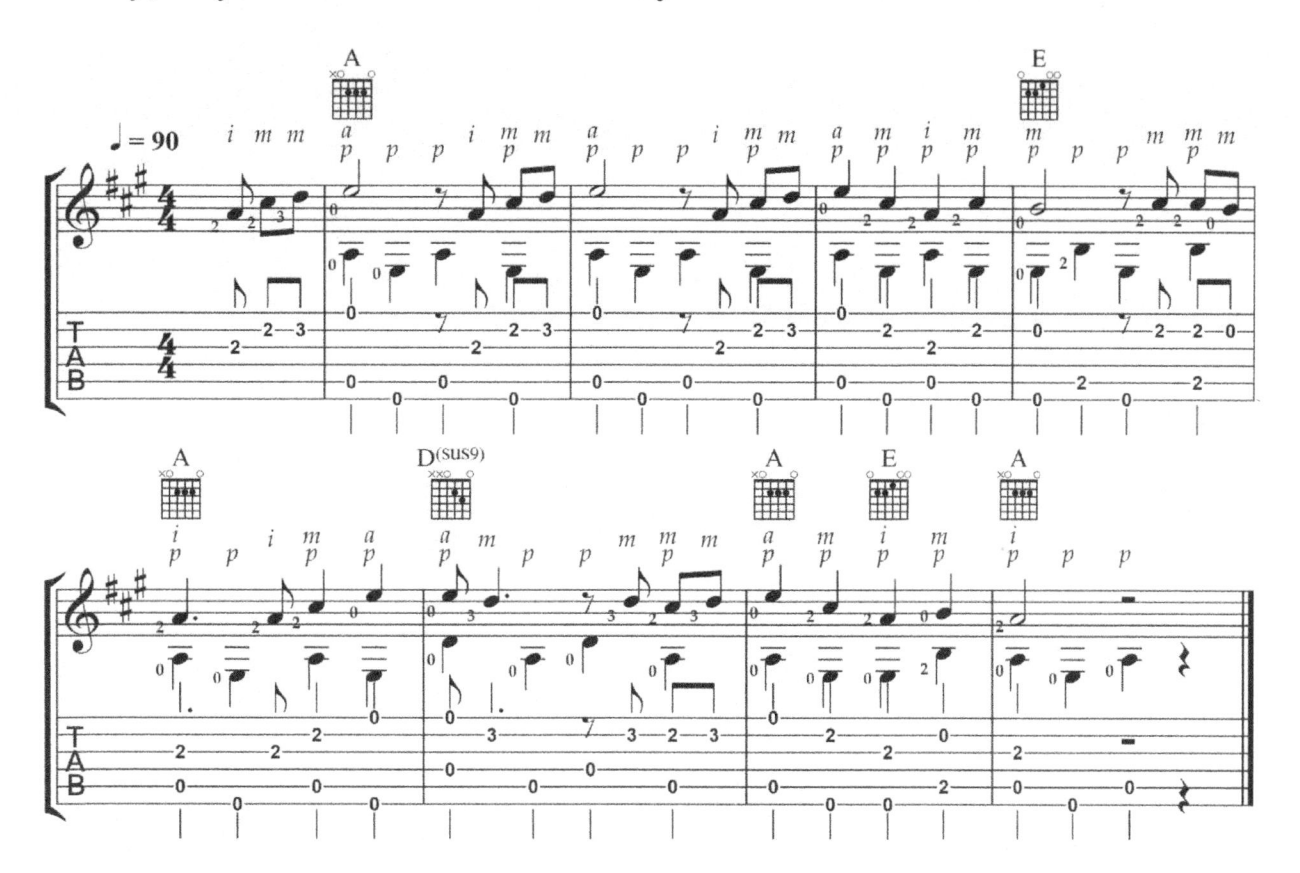

Conclusion

Congratulations on finishing level 6. You've stepped up your fingerpicking game, learned a legendary bass pattern, and even played two full songs. Not bad for a single level! That was a lot to chew on, so feel free to come back to any of the exercises and practice them slowly with a metronome.

Let's keep moving and I'll teach you to play in the style of famous fingerpicking guitar players!

Level 7

~ 4 days ~

Essential Techniques

You're approaching the end of this book. But before going out on the wild alone, I'll show you a few guitar techniques that you're likely to find in fingerstyle guitar tunes. For each technique, there will be some exercises to practice so that you can internalize it. You might know some or all of these, but it's always a good idea to practice them in isolation to make sure you get them right.

Let's dive in.

Hammer-on

A hammer-on consists of sharply fretting a note *after* plucking the string, instead of before plucking the string. This creates a note sound that is less audible and less bright, and it misses the attack of the right-hand finger.

Hammer-ons are used not only because of the sound they produce but because they allow us to play fast, easily. Since the left hand is the only one needed to create a note, this frees the right hand. And since there's no need to coordinate both as in a regular plucked note, it's easier to play fast successions of notes.

This technique requires you to swiftly apply some strength on the fret with your left hand. If you can't get it to sound, try to press the finger closer to the fret (the metal bar). This can take some practice and you'll maybe have to build a bit of left hand muscle strength. Yet, in order to avoid unnecessary muscle tension, I recommend you to apply the strength needed to perform the hammer-on and no more. As with all other guitar techniques, the ideal hammer-on is effective and precise, yet effortless. This will come with practice.

The hammer-on is represented by the "legato" lines connecting two or more higher notes. This means that the first note among these has to be plucked, while the following notes included in the line should be played with the hammer-on technique.

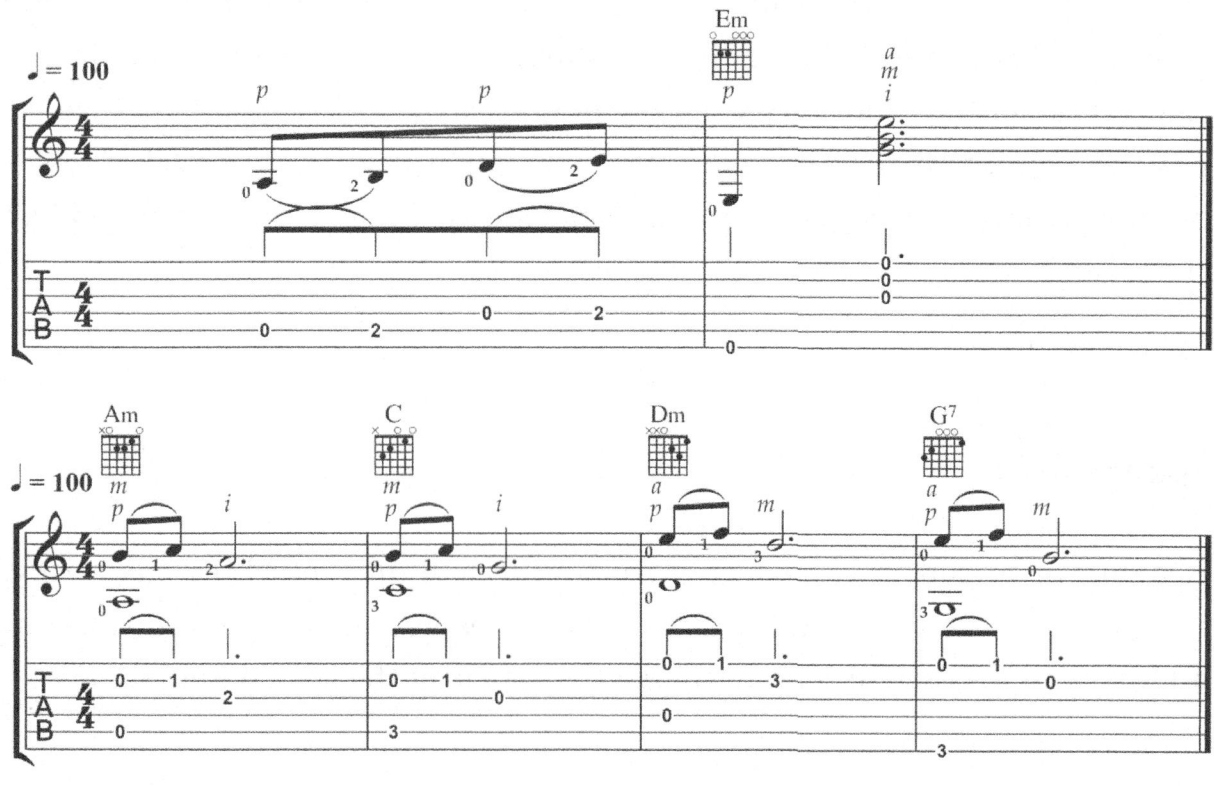

Hammer-ons allow you to easily make normal chords more interesting by momentarily adding additional notes that add color to the chord.

Here we're adding a 9th on every chord with a hammer-on, turning the common C - Am - Dm - G into the colorful Cadd9 - Amadd - Dmadd9 - Gadd9.

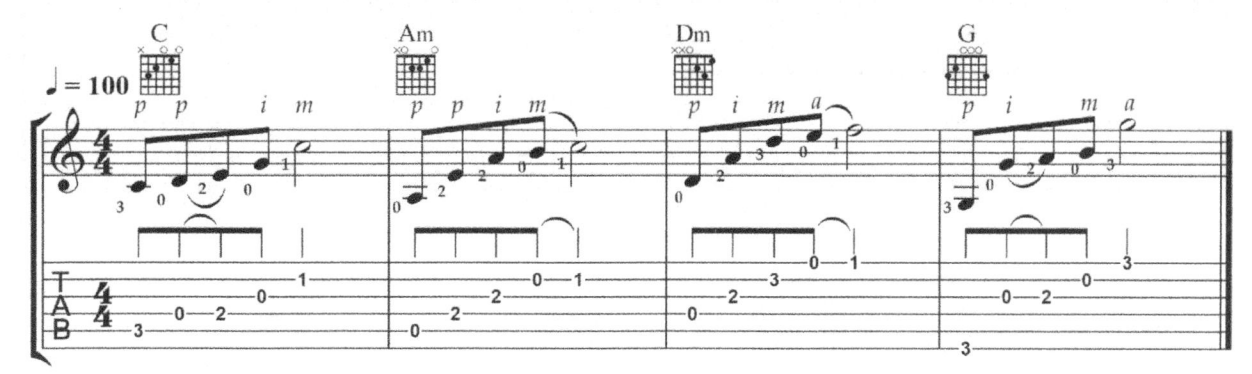

Pull-off

The pull-off is the dark side of the hammer-on. Well, not really the dark side, but definitely the opposite. While a hammer-on consists of fretting a higher note on an already vibrating string, a pull-off means fretting a *lower note*. The result is similar to the hammer-on: less audible notes that allow you to play faster while freeing your right hand.

As in the hammer-on, a pull-off is also indicated by legato lines, but this time the following notes are lower than the first one instead of higher. When you see this, pluck the first note pull-off the following notes included within the legato line.

To make it work, you have to take off the finger quickly and decisively. It can be a tad trickier than a hammer-on, but practice will make it better.

Enough talking, try to pull off these pull-offs!

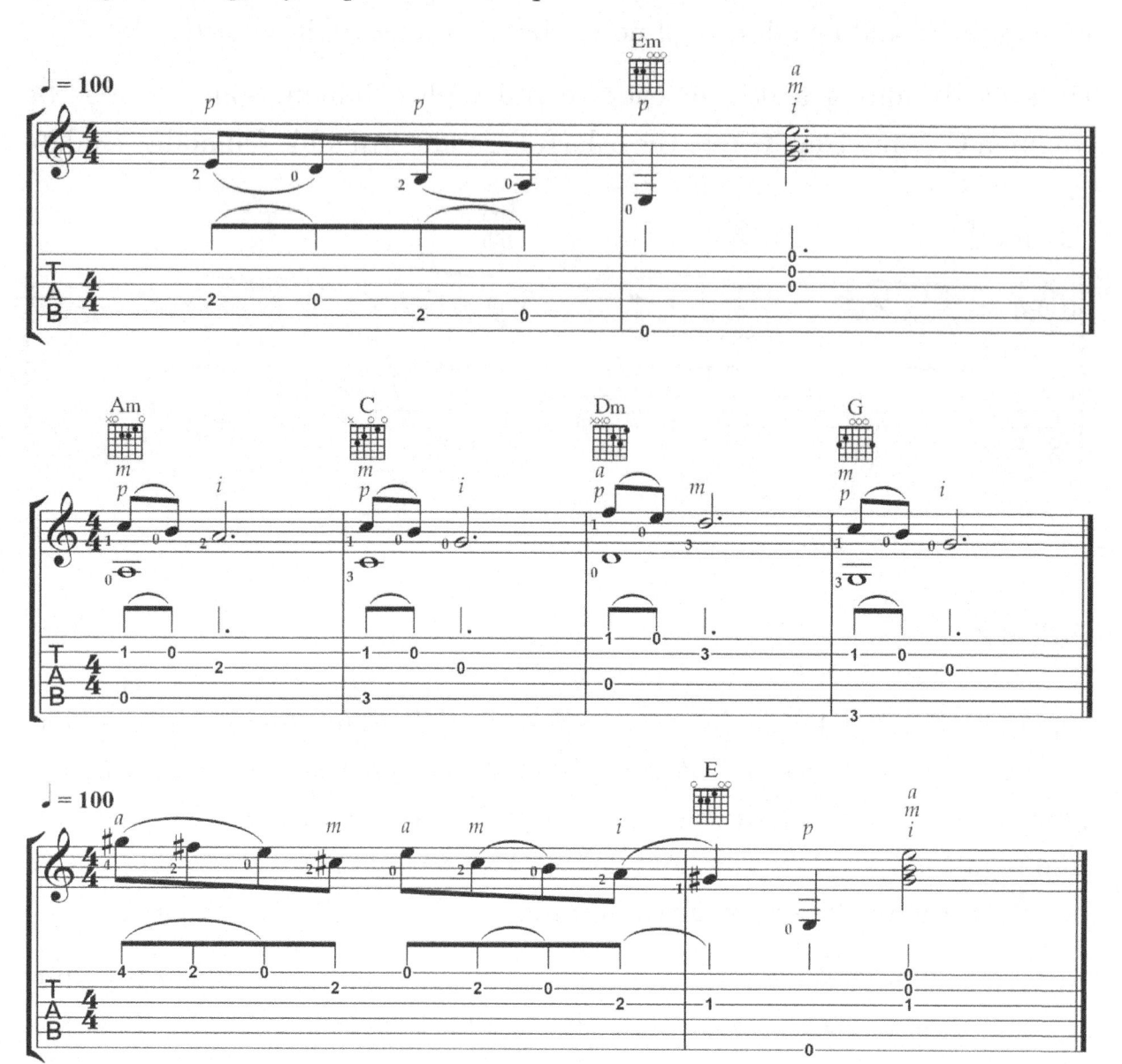

Harmonics

If you pluck string 6 open and you let it ring for a while, you'll hear how the lower frequencies of the note fade out, leaving only some seemingly higher-pitch residual note. What you're hearing is some of the harmonics of the initial note.

There are some interesting physical phenomena going in here, but as much as I'd like it, turning you into a scientist isn't in the scope of this book. What you have to keep in mind, though, is that harmonics are high-pitched and that they're "hiding" within every note you play.

The interesting part is that you can trigger these harmonics immediately to achieve that soft-sounding high-pitch as if it was a normal note. There are different ways to do so, but the most effective one is to use "natural harmonics".

Natural harmonics happen when you lightly touch the 12th fret - right *on top* of the metallic bar - with your a left hand finger and pluck the string with your right hand, then you immediately lift your left hand to let the string ring. Keep in mind that your left hand shouldn't really fret the fretboard, but just very lightly touch the string on top of the metallic fret (instead of next to the fret as when you fret normal notes).

The resulting sound will be a soft-sounding, high-pitch note: what you're doing here is like playing an open string but muting part of the sound so that only the harmonics remain.

The tricky part is that the moment you pluck the string, you have to *immediately* lift your finger or you'll kill the harmonics. You can produce natural harmonics by placing the finger on the 12th fret - these are the easiest to play - but also on the 5th and 7th frets. There are some other spots where you can do that, but the resulting harmonics are very weak and they're rarely used. Harmonics can also be played on various strings at the same time, all on the same fret. For example, on the 12th fret of strings 1, 2, and 3 at once - you can do that by slightly touching the strings as usual but this time as if you were about to do a barre chord with the index.

Playing harmonics is difficult at first and requires a lot of trial and error. But when you do it right... you're going to impress. Spice them with care over a tune and they will surprise your audience with an unexpected and refreshing sound.

In the following exercises, harmonics are represented with the *harm.* word and all notes within the dotted lines should be also played as harmonics.

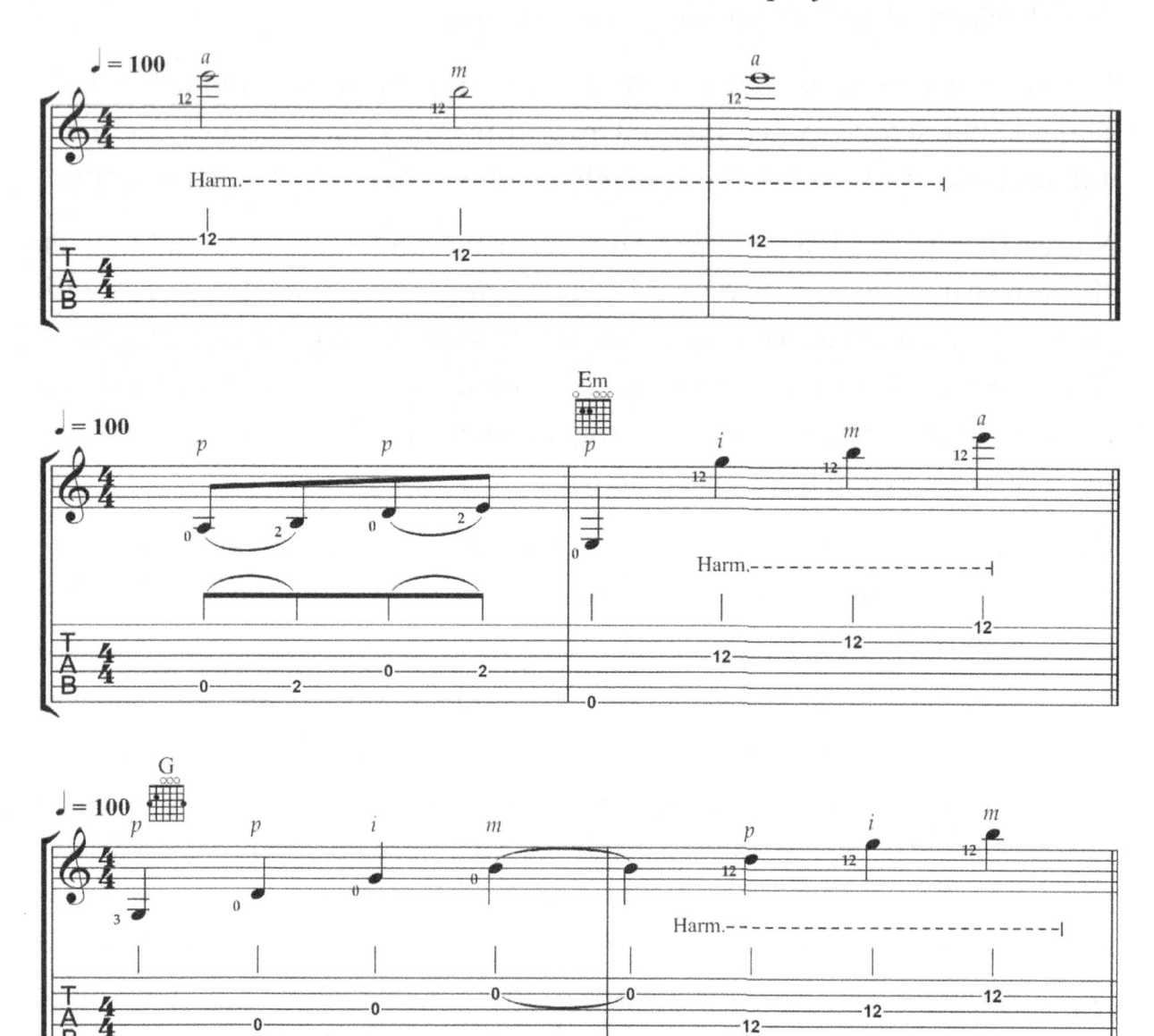

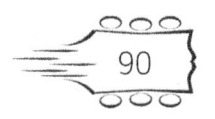

Slapping thumb

Adding percussive elements to guitar parts is one of the most fascinating things in fingerpicking guitar for many. A lot of modern fingerpicking guitarists use it to add momentum to their songs, and it's often a surprising touch that catches audiences off-guard.

Slapping your thumb on the strings sounds similar to the snare of a drumkit, and like such, it's often used on the 2nd and 4th beat of every bar. Combined with the basslines we previously learned how to play, adding percussive elements to your fingerpicking can create the impression of a one-man-band: you've got a bass, you've got drums, and on top of that you can add melodies, arpeggios, and chords. Normally when you slap the string you kill any bass note playing on that string, so getting the right combination of bass notes and slapping is crucial to get a satisfying result.

The thumb slap is represented by a cross in the exercises below. Hit the string with the cross with the flesh at the side of your thumb (not with your nail) and keep it there for the duration of the whole note.

In this one, slap the string on beats two and four.

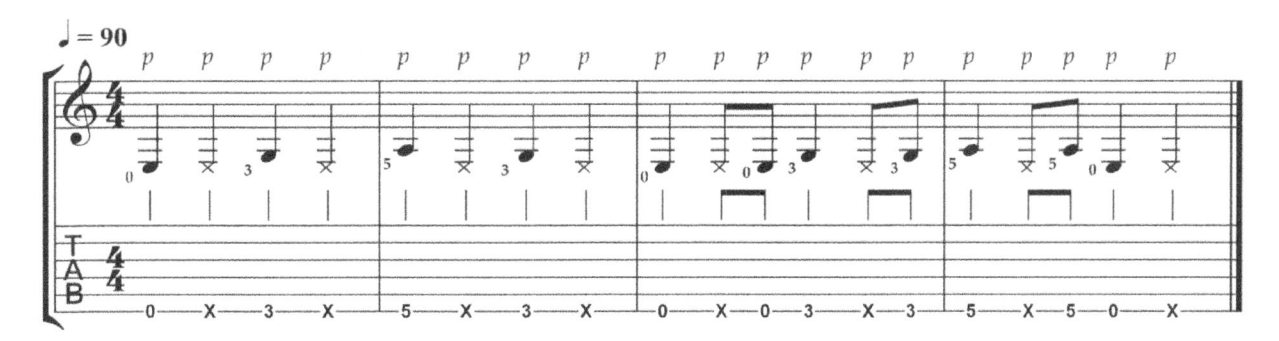

Now a similar one but with two differences: The whole bassline and slapping are played on string 5 instead of string 6, and now there are chords in between bass notes and slapping. This makes for a very interesting rhythm, very useful as background for vocals.

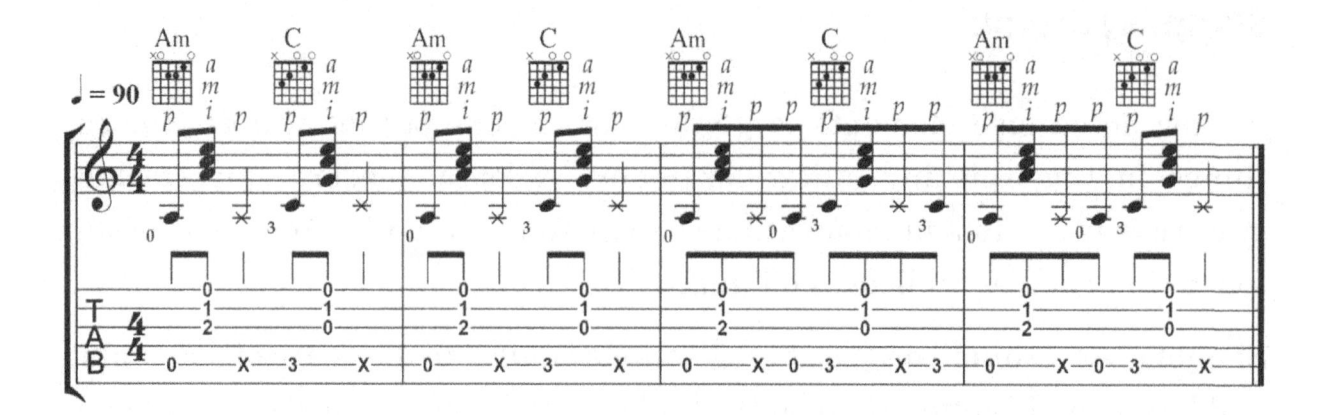

Now let's try to combine arpeggios and thumb slapping. It's like a normal arpeggio but every second thumb note is a slap instead of a normal note. In this case, the thumb slap falls on beat four of every bar.

Thumb slapping is also very useful when strumming chords or plucking the all at once.

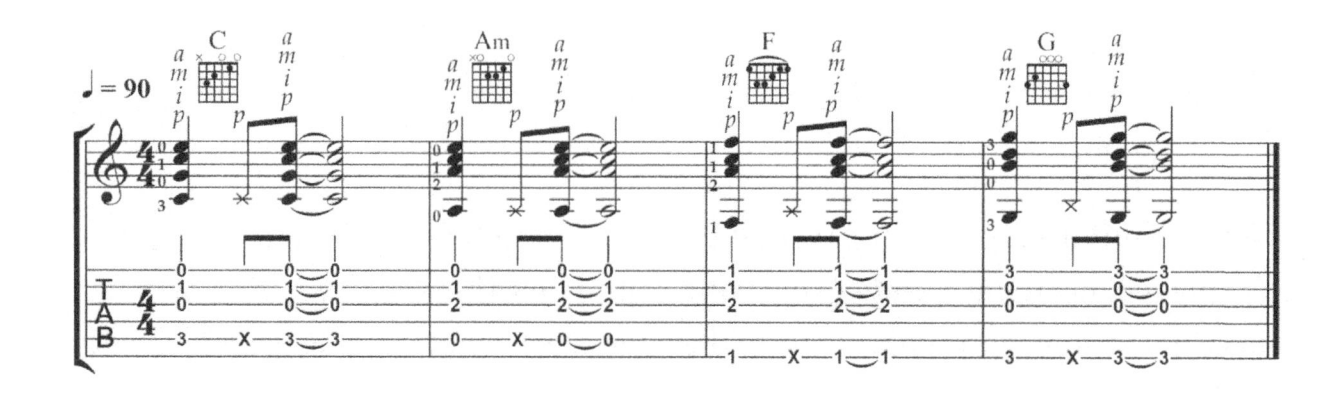

And the last one, this time slapping the string only on the second beat of every bar. We could slap it on the fourth beat too, but then we wouldn't be able to play a bass note. In this case I've chosen to keep the bass note.

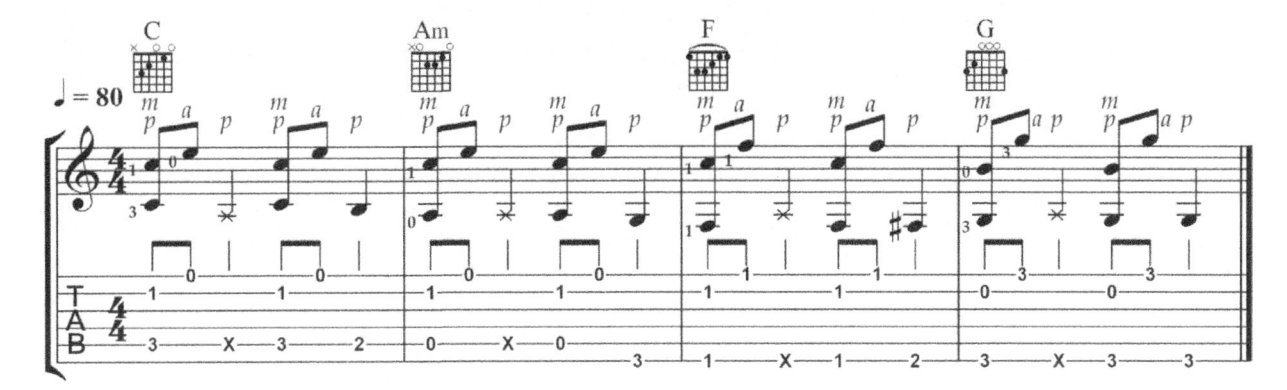

Conclusion

When playing fingerpicking guitar, there are many ways in which the same musical idea can be played. The guitar techniques we've just seen will expand the way in which you can do so. If you play fingerpicking songs or arrangements by others, these techniques will allow you to play almost any song you encounter. If you make your own songs or arrangements, your personal taste - acquired through practice - will show you when to use each of these techniques to bring your ideas to life in the most interesting ways.

We're reaching the big finale. See you in the next part.

PART 2
KEEP YOUR JOURNEY GOING

Chapter 1

Licks In The Style Of Greats

Fingerpicking guitar can be played in many ways. In this chapter, we're going to take a look at the style of famous fingerpicking guitar players, with a few exercises for each that imitate their peculiarities.

Travis Picking

Travis Picking is a legendary fingerpicking pattern created by Merle Travis. It's a steady stream of alternating notes that has a distinctive Folk/Country sound. It's often played as a bassline, with melodies and chords playing on top of it. It creates a lot of momentum and it's a very effective way to bring life to a chord progression.

Travis Picking is used a lot in fingerpicking guitar, so it's worth memorizing it well. Practice it again and again until your thumb knows how to play it instinctively. Once you get there, playing chords and melodies on top of it will be easy breezy.

It's usually played palm muted. Let's give it a try - this is the basic pattern on C.

In the same way that we can use an arpeggio pattern on many different chords, the Travis Picking bass pattern can be used on almost any chord you can think of.

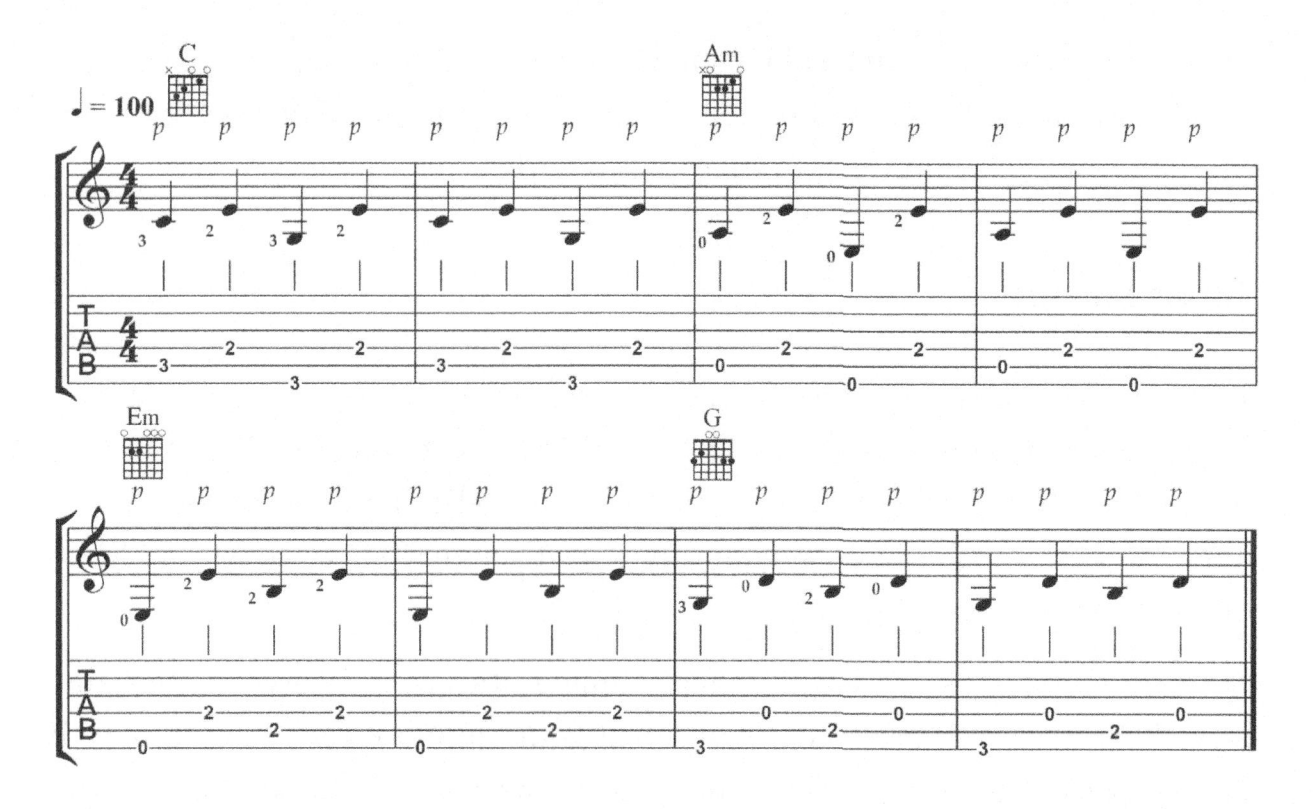

Travis Picking is often played with chords and/or melodies on top of it. Palm mute the bass notes and let ring the higher notes.

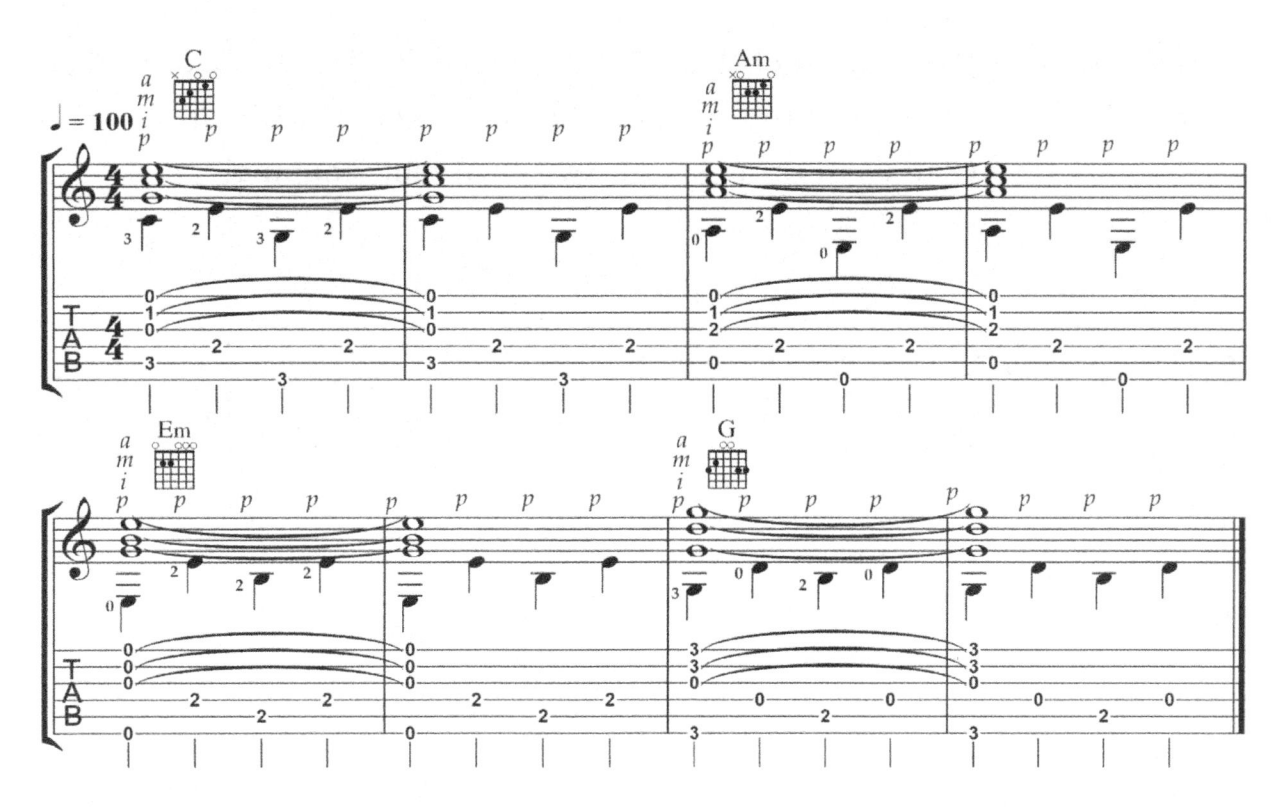

Let's try the same Travis Picking bass pattern, but this time with a simple melody on top instead of chords.

And now with a syncopated melody, as it's common with Travis Picking. Start slow with a metronome and repeat it until you can play it without mistakes at 120bpm. If you can do it, try to play it twice without stopping!

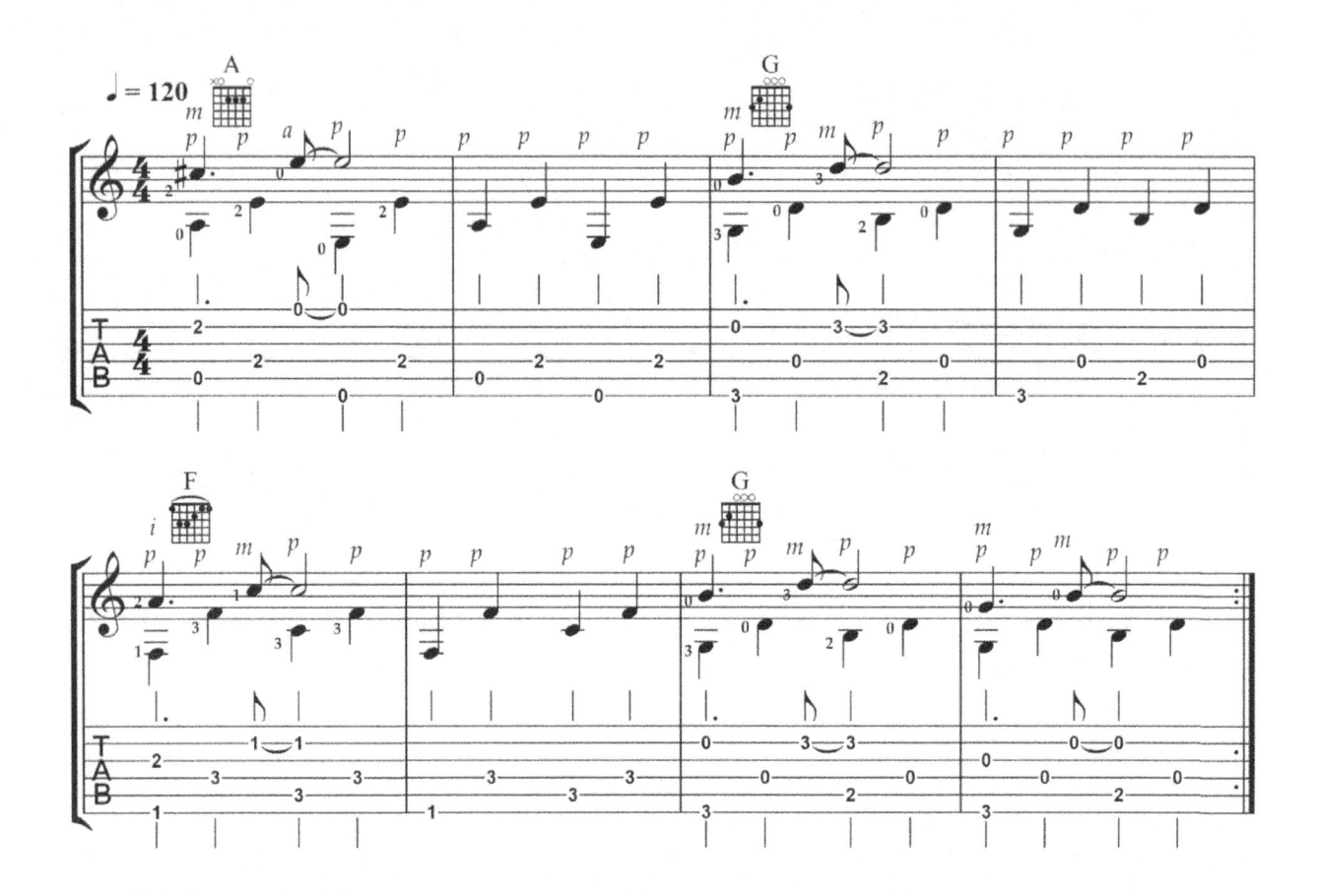

> Check the bonus section to hear these exercises in the style of the greats.

James Taylor

James Taylor is an influential singer-songwriter. He uses his guitar to accompany his voice, so his style is well suited to accommodate vocals, mixing arpeggios and strummed chords.

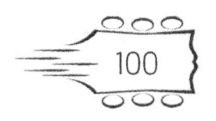

Simon & Garfunkel

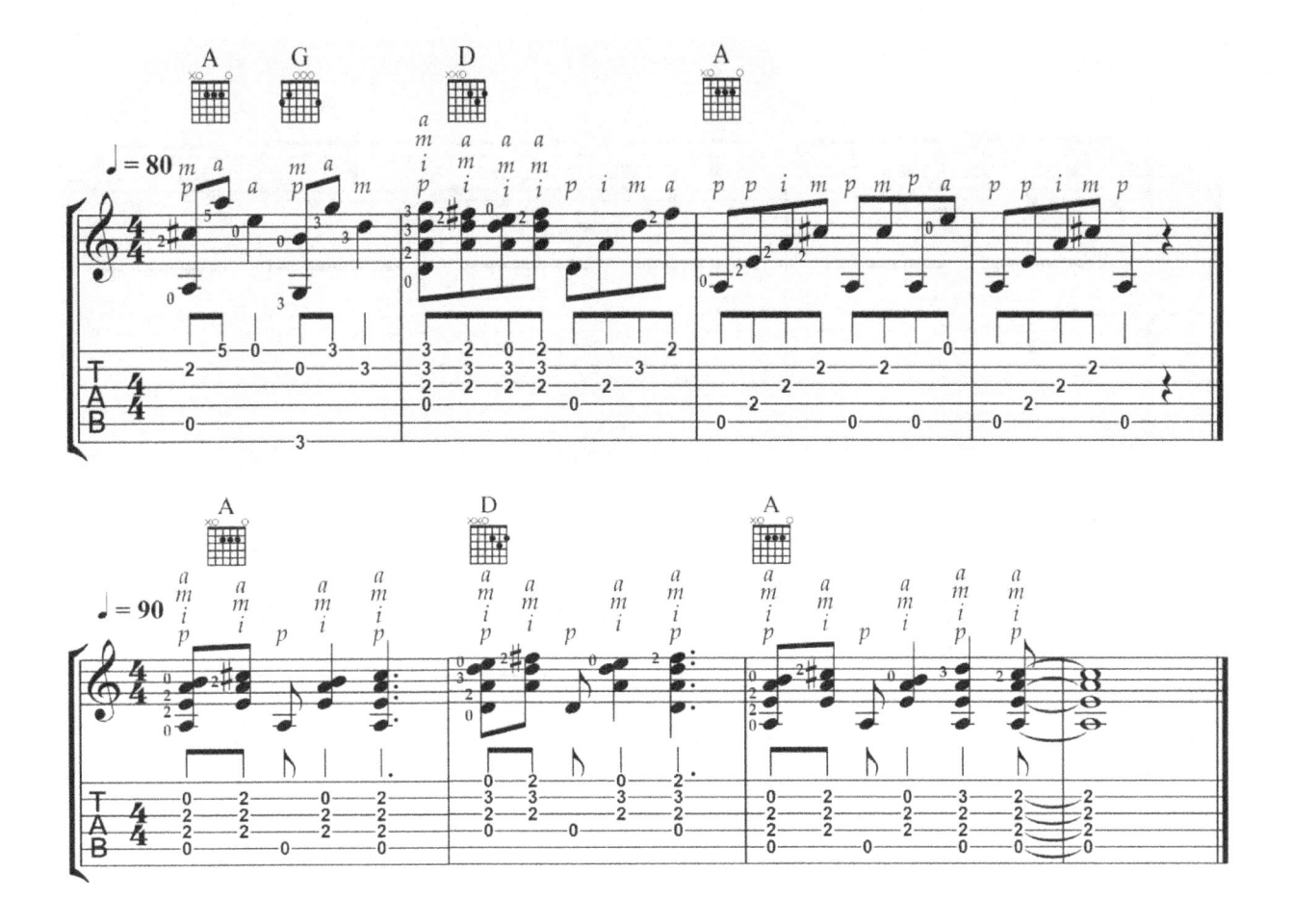

Simon & Garfunkel were a legendary American folk rock duo. The guitar parts they used as accompaniment were clearly folk but often surprisingly atmospheric. Check out these two exercises to get a glimpse of their style.

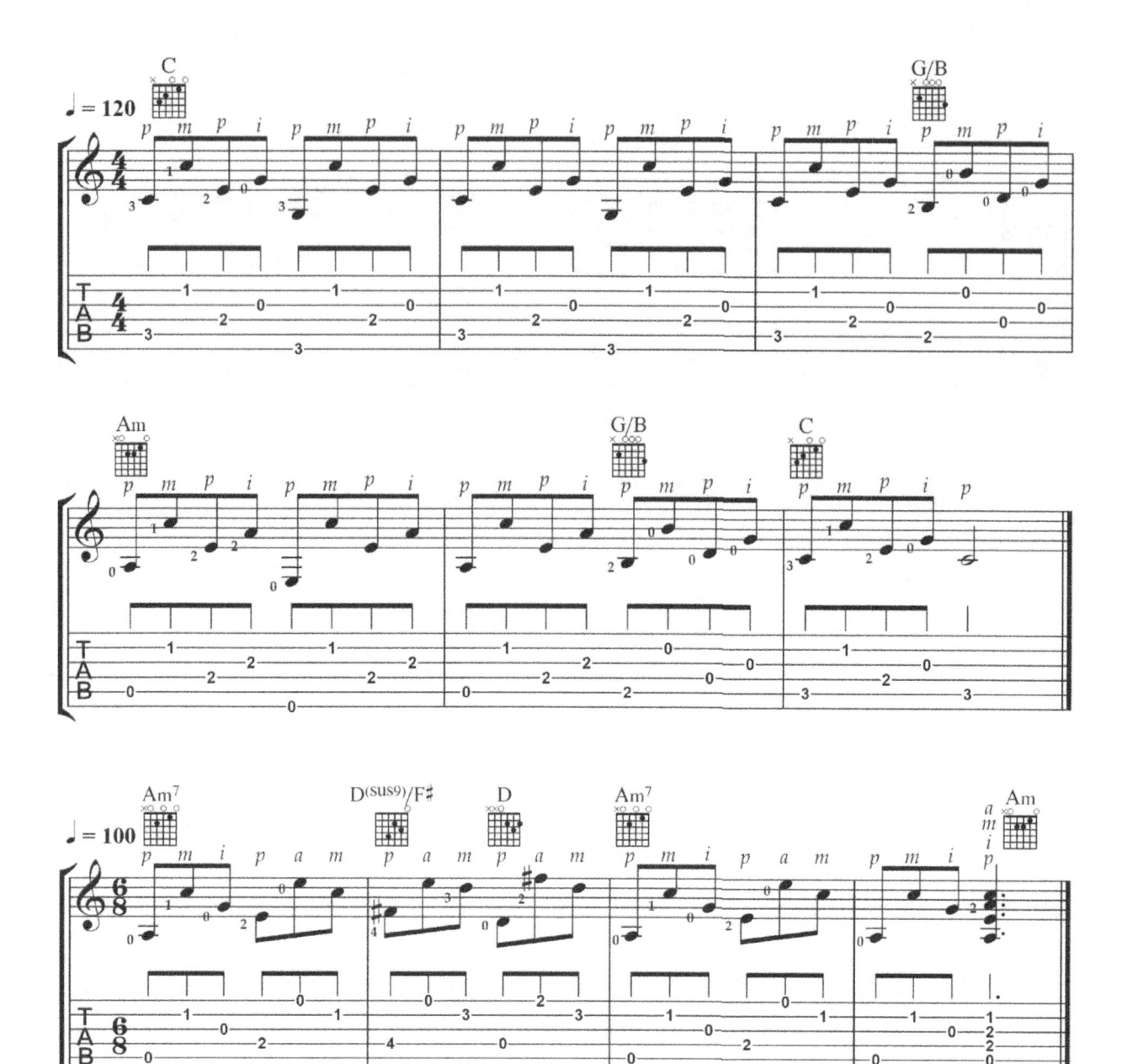

Chet Atkins

A guitar legend, Chet Atkins took Travis Picking (first created by guitarist Merle Travis) and brought it to new heights, creating practically a music style on its own rooted on Country and with Jazz influences. He's been and still is a big influence on many fingerpicking guitar players, including Tommy

Emmanuel, whom we'll see in a moment.

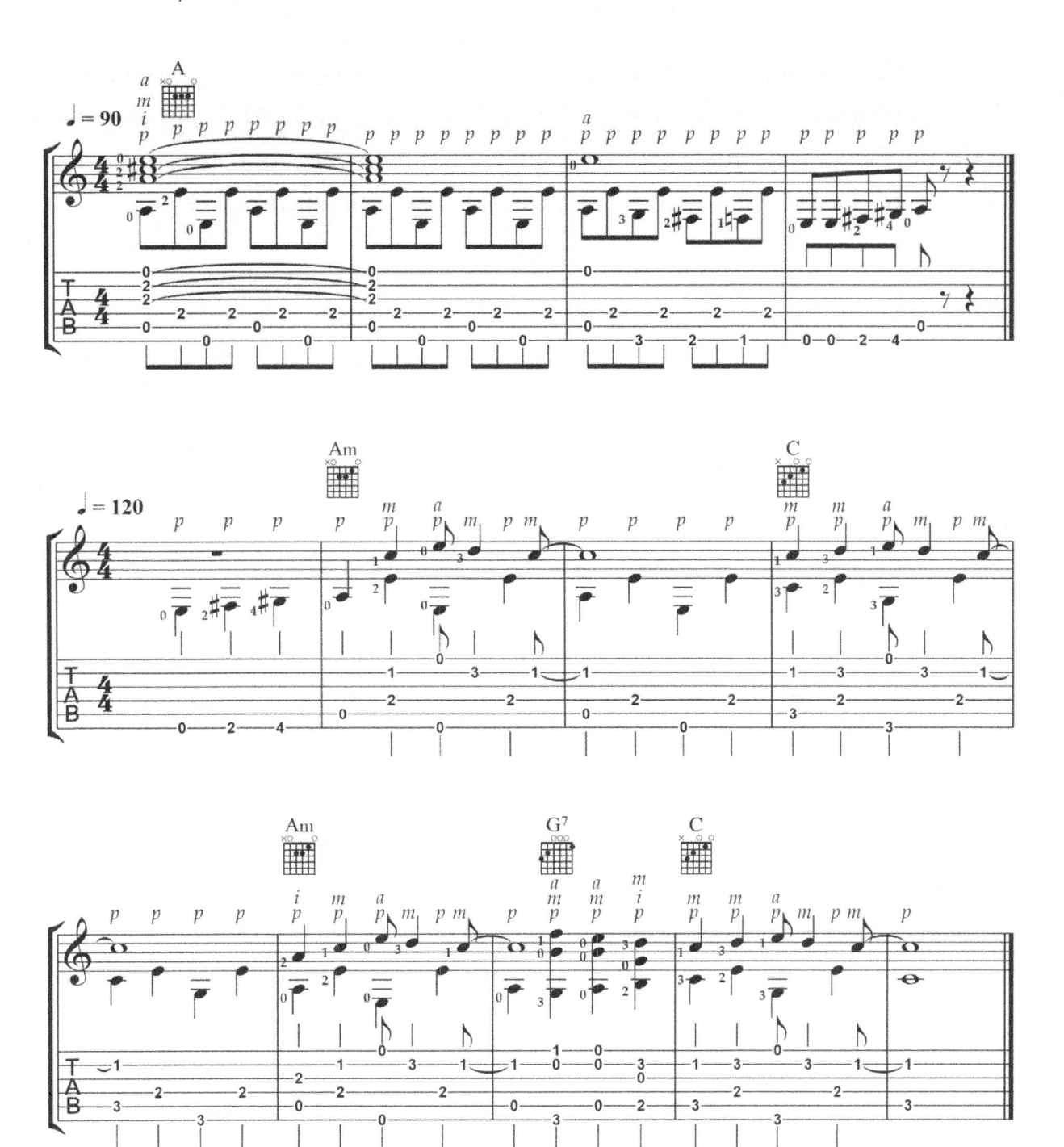

Tommy Emmanuel

Tommy Emmanuel is a living legend of immense popularity. His style is clearly influenced by Chet Atkins, but he's also a master of adding surprises in his performance. This, combined with his high energy and stage presence, turned him into one of the most respected fingerstyle guitar players.

Mauro Giuliani

Mauro Giuliani was an Italian classical guitar player and composer, and his etudes are still praised by nowadays classical guitar players.

I'm going to show you a few classical studies based on his style. Why? Because it's a great way to learn how to play fingerpicking guitar in a classical way. Whether you're eager to enjoy the delicacies of classical guitar or anything older than the XX century makes you fall asleep, these etudes will improve your playing, which will be reflected in any style you play.

The first four will be simple exercises for the right hand. These will improve the coordination of your right hand fingers.

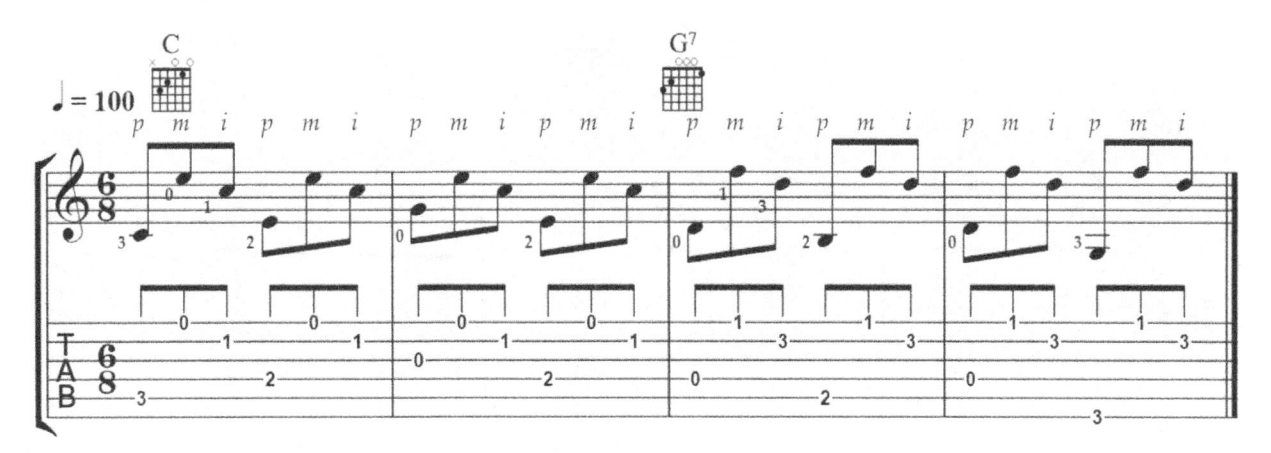

As you'll see, these four exercises all use practically the same left hand fingering, so that you can focus on your right hand.

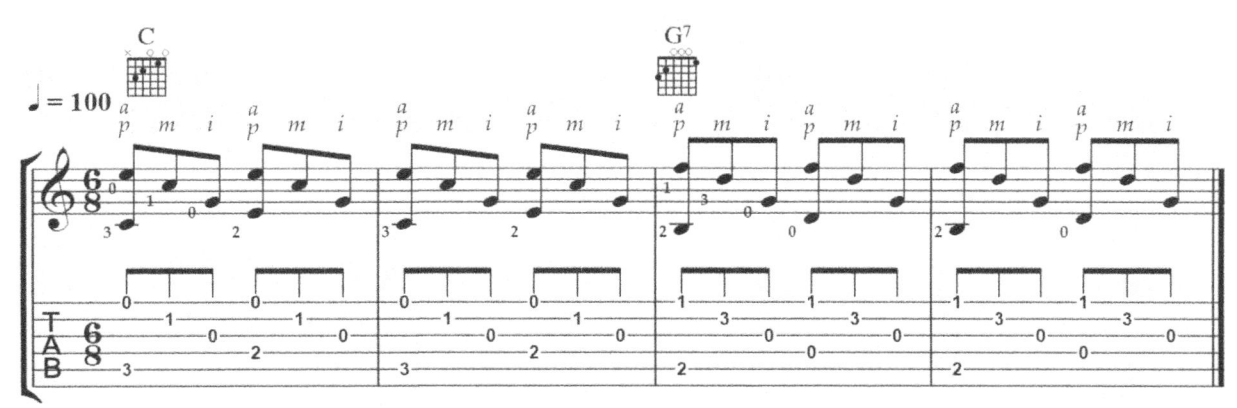

Let's increase the difficulty a bit. Let those strings ring as much as you can.

Now with a different pattern on strings 1 and 2.

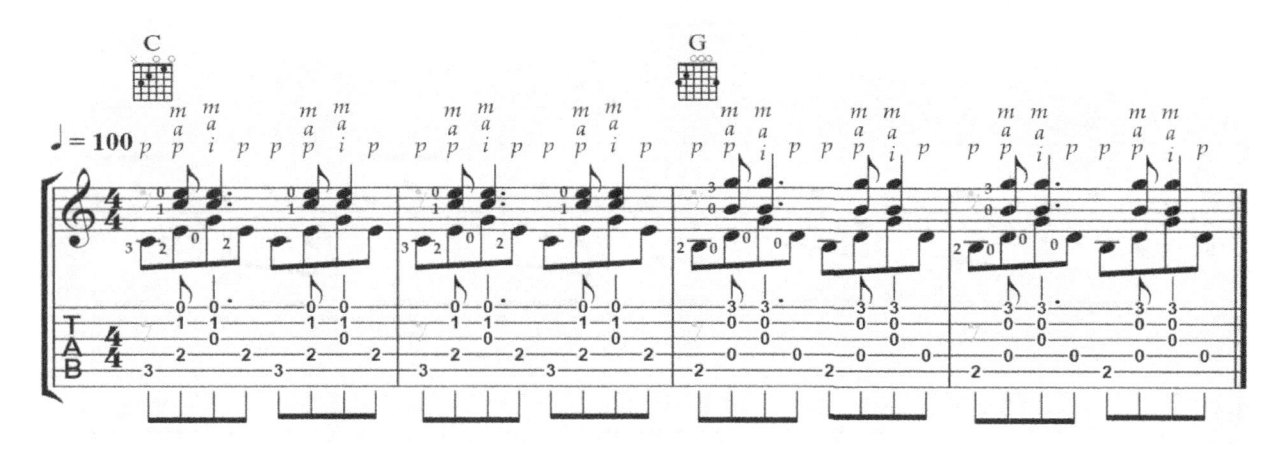

Let's dive into more complex studies - these kind of studies are great to improve your technique. The next one has two melodic lines. Instead of having a solid bassline and a melody on top of it, as it's common in modern music, the bassline in this study sounds rather like a melody on its own, answering to the higher pitch main melody. This is not uncommon in classical guitar pieces.

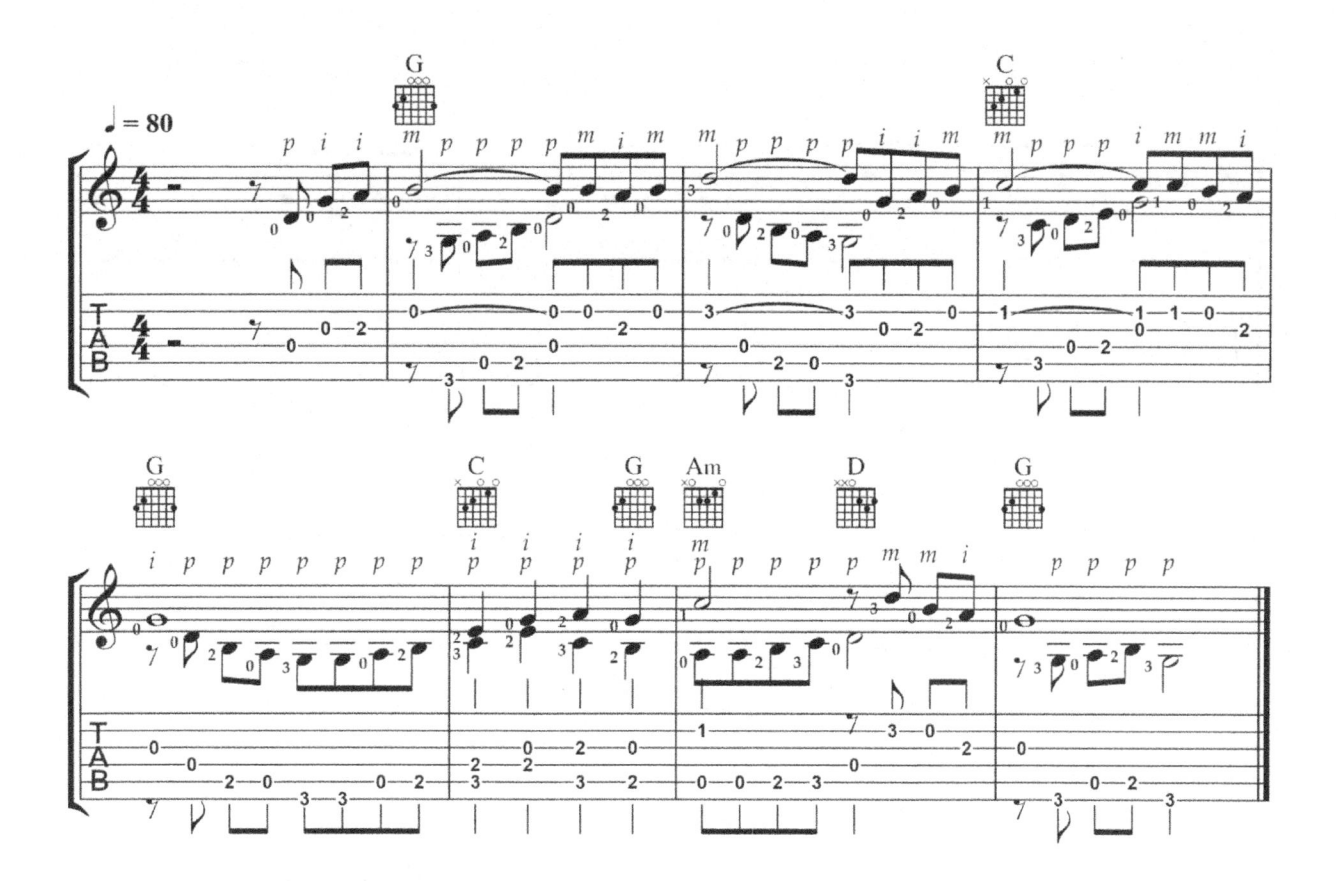

The second study doesn't have a clear melody but the bassline has a fair amount of movement.

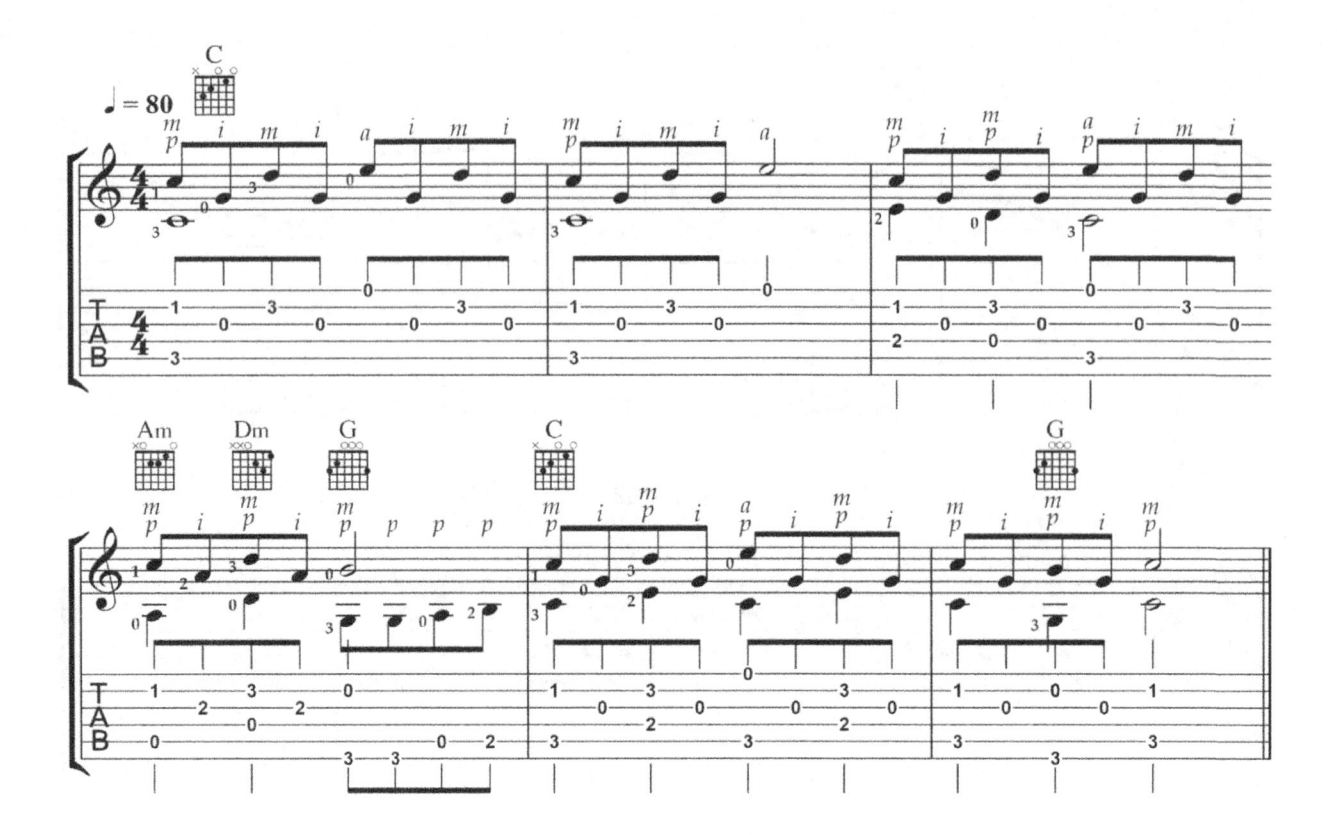

The next study, the third one, is a series of beautiful dark arpeggios in a 6/8 time signature.

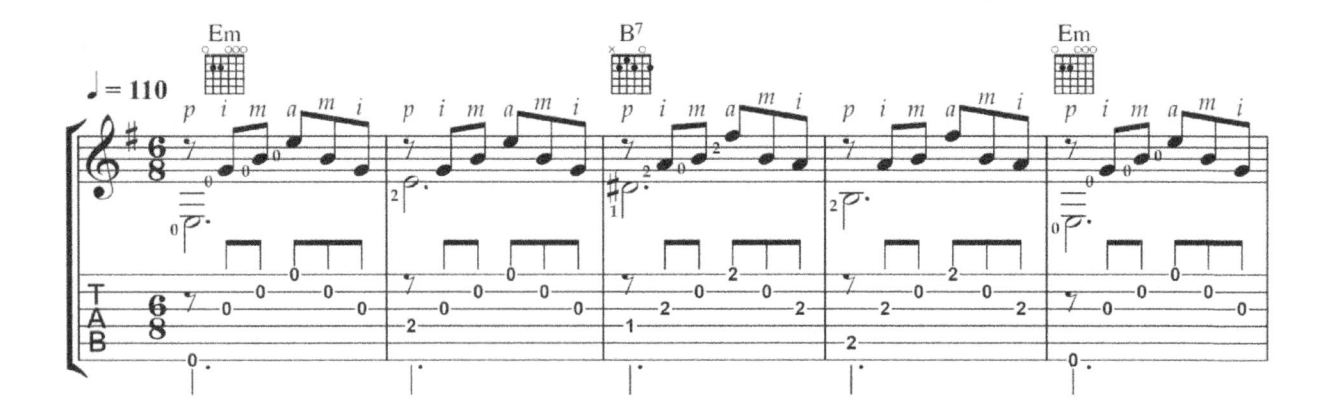

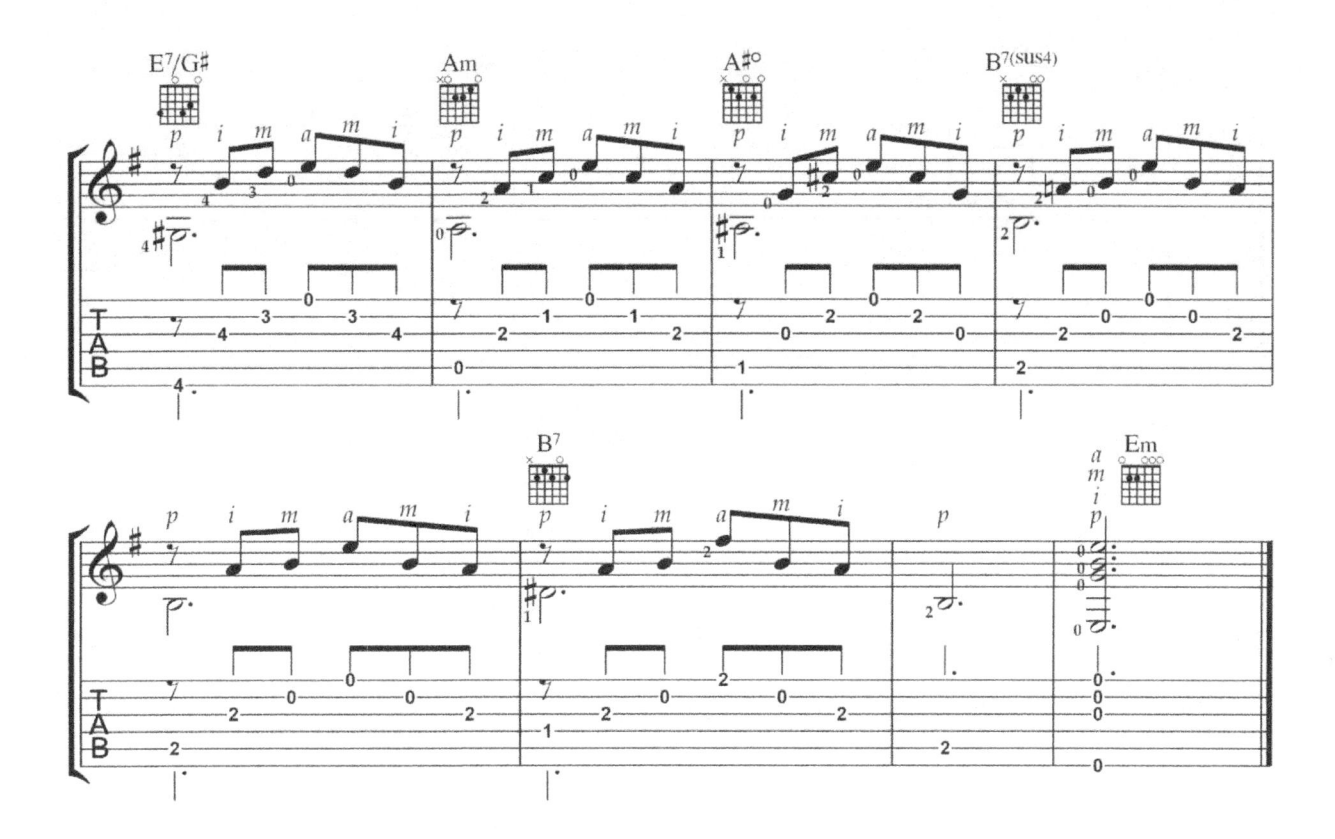

And the last one is also in a 6/8 time signature and also quite dark, but this time with more energy. Remember the fermata we saw when we played the fingerpicking version of "Happy Birthday"? You'll find it again here, before the last part. Keep that chord longer than expected to create tension before resolving it in the last chord. Make it dramatic!

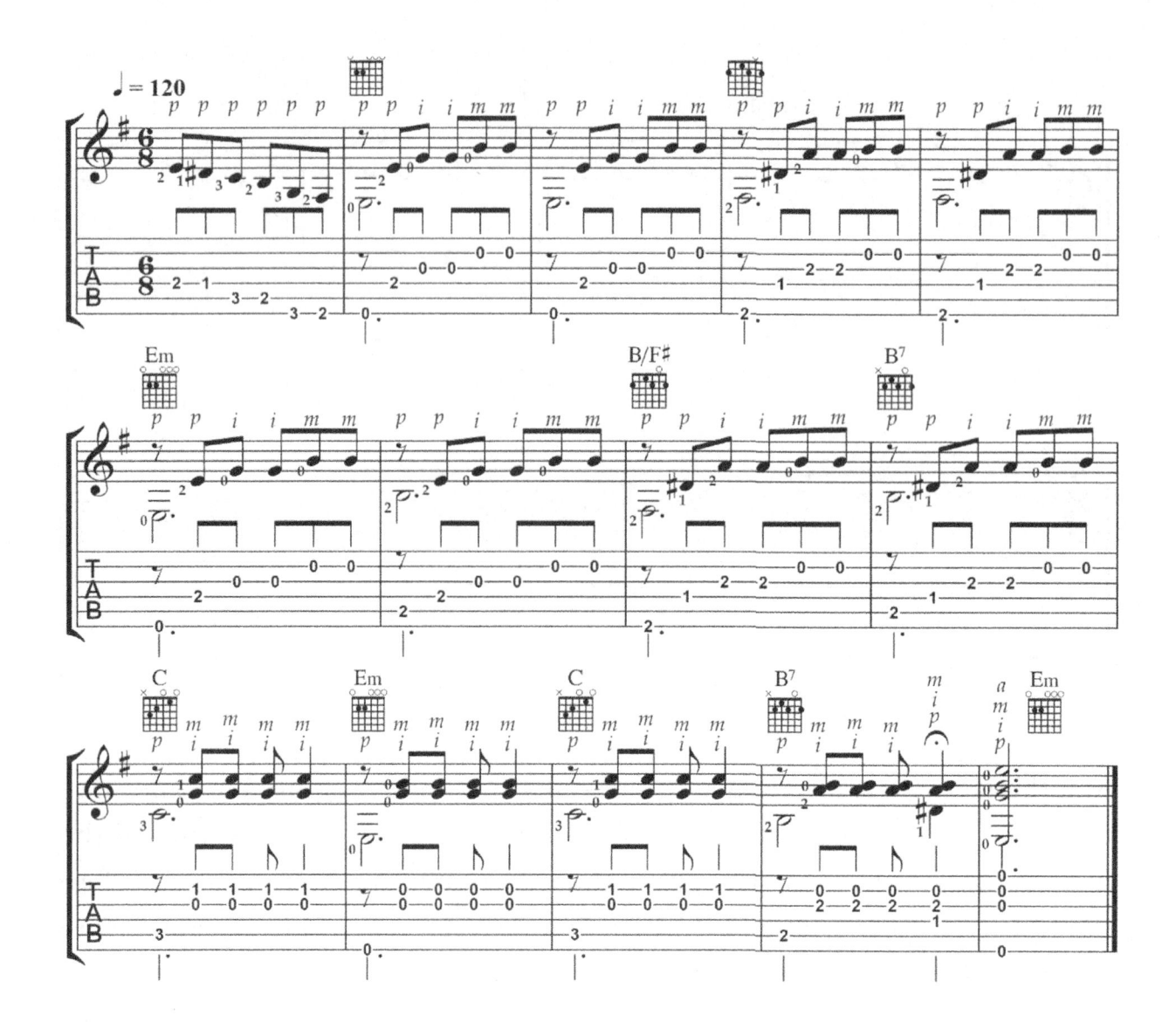

Fingerstyle guitar

Conclusion

While it's important to learn the basics of fingerstyle guitar, studying the peculiarities and techniques of the greatest can give us a lot of ideas and inspiration. Each of the guitar players we've scene has its own style, to the point where you could often recognize them just from the way the play.

As you advance in your path as a fingerstyle guitar player, you will also develop your own style, prioritizing certain techniques above others, guided by your own taste. But first we have to dig deeper into the possibilities your guitar offers. Move on to the next chapter to discover them!

Chapter 2

More Pieces

You've really gotten far! You've been through a learning journey full of techniques, tips, and exercises - and it's time to put it all together for you to shine.

I'd like you to take your time to practice and play the three fingerpicking tunes in this chapter. With them, you will consolidate all you've learned in this book. If you can play them at the recommended tempo, you will have a very strong foundation to play fingerpicking guitar and you'll be able to learn any song you want.

If you feel overwhelmed and you feel like this is too much for you, don't fret. Fingerpicking guitar songs *are* hard at first. They can be intimidating, with so many notes played at the same time. But you're not supposed to be pulling them of in a breeze. Songs take time to be played properly and these below aren't an exception. use a metronome, start very slow (even if you think it's ridiculously slow), and repeat, repeat, repeat.

It's normal to feel frustrated at first, but that's part of the magic. Few things in life are as satisfying as mastering a song that seemed impossible at first.

Here you have the songs. As in previous ones, I've added versions with only the bassline and only the melody so that you can try them separately before putting them together.

Have fun!

Camp Town Races

"Camp Town Races" is a widely known American folk song from the mid-1800s, written by Stephen Foster. The following fingerpicking version of this catchy tune will test your abilities with Travis Picking.

Let's take a look at the isolated Travis Picking bassline first. Play it all palm muted.

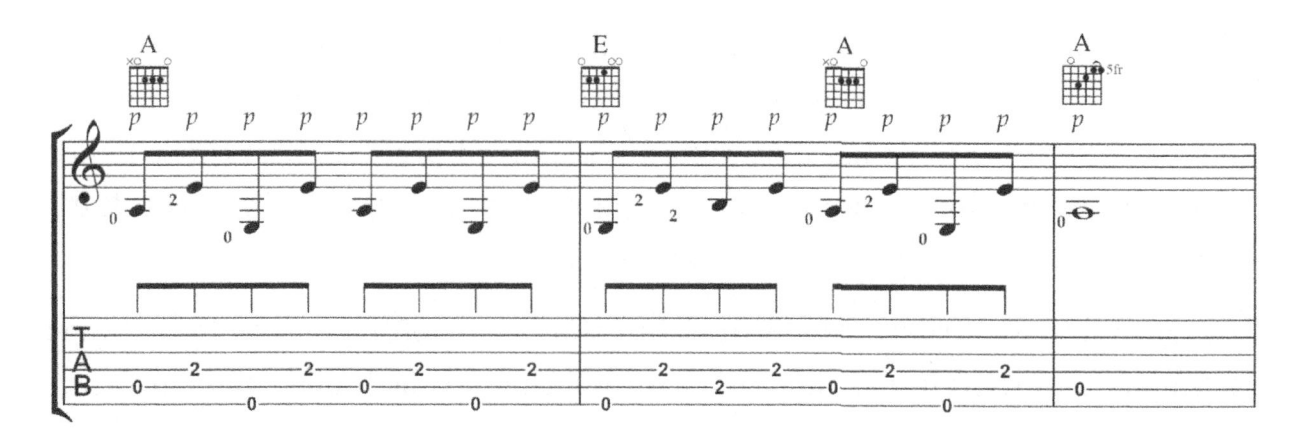

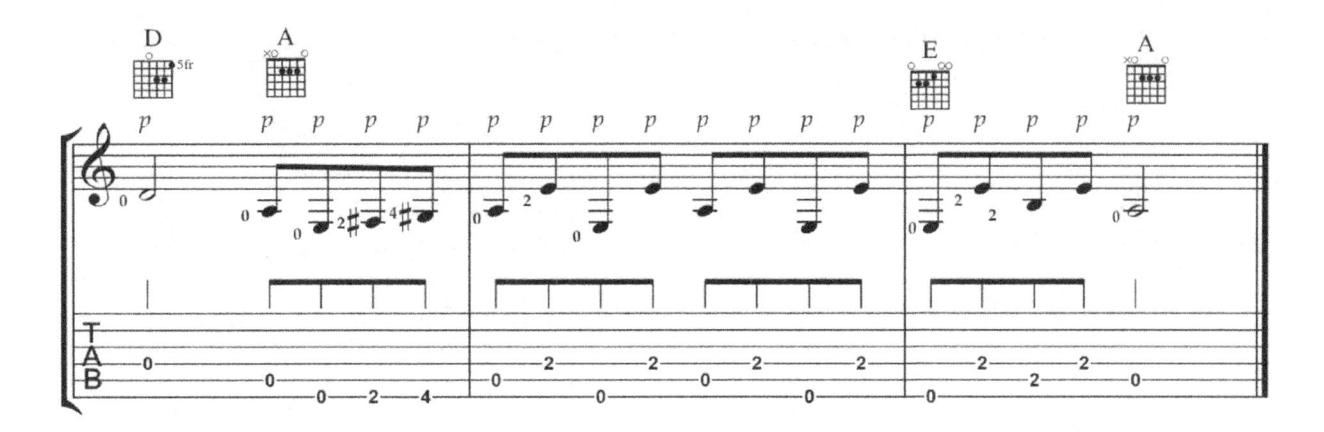

Here comes the isolated melody.

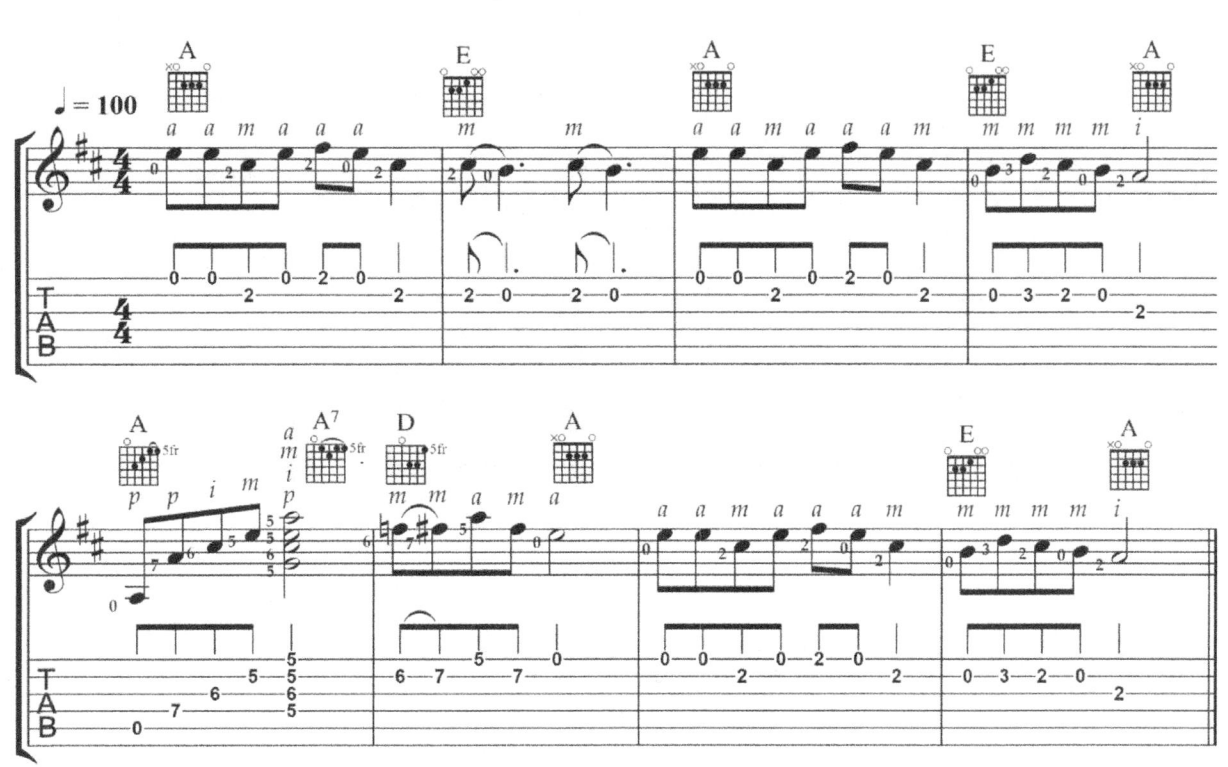

Fingerstyle guitar

And now the full version, with everything together.

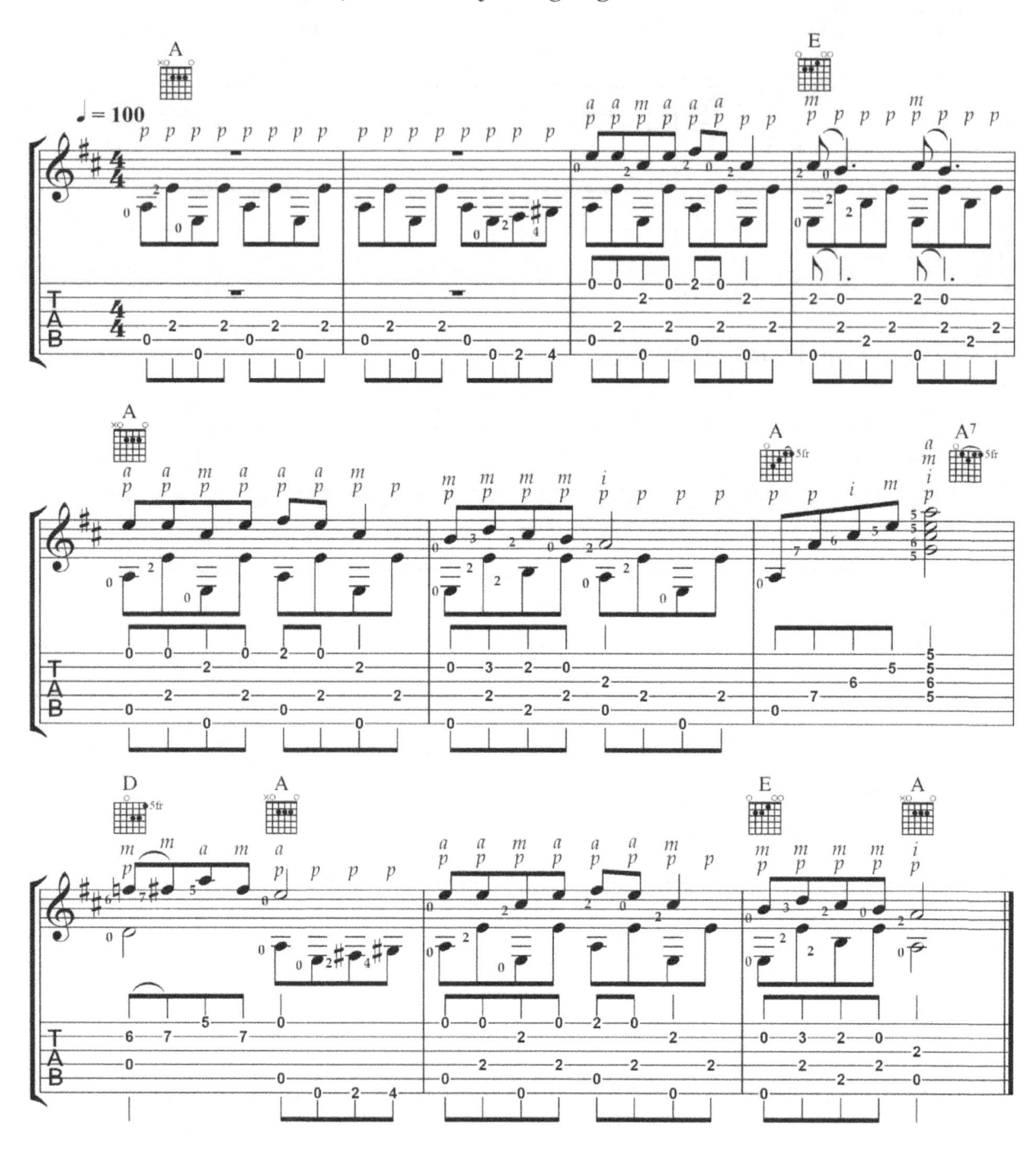

Auld Lang Syne

"Auld Lang Syne" is an old song in the Scots language, nowadays associated with New Year's Eve. It's a well-known song, however, the following fingerpicking has a twist: it has percussion, played by slapping the thumb on the second beat of every bar.

Here you have the bassline and thumb slapping only.

Now the iconic melody, with harmonics on the 5th bar.

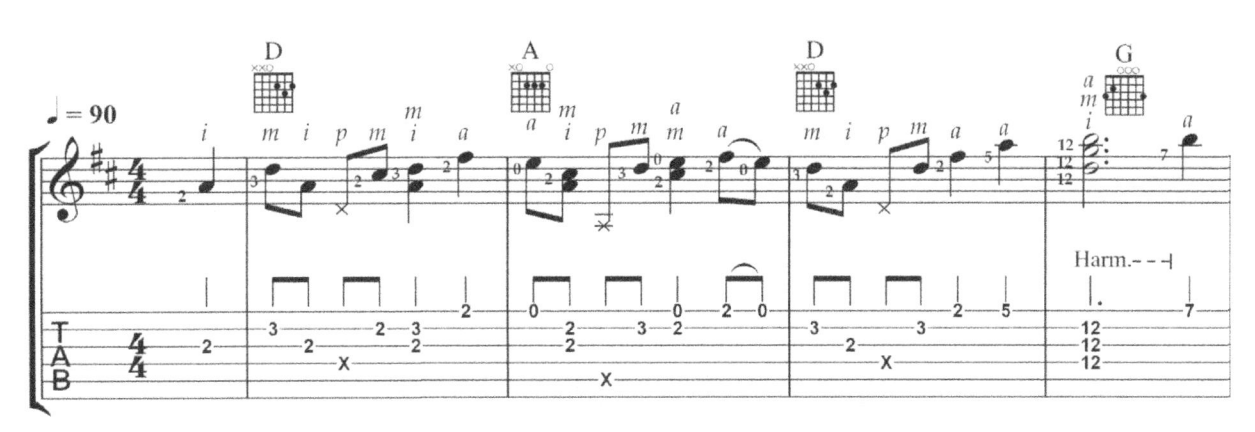

Fingerstyle guitar

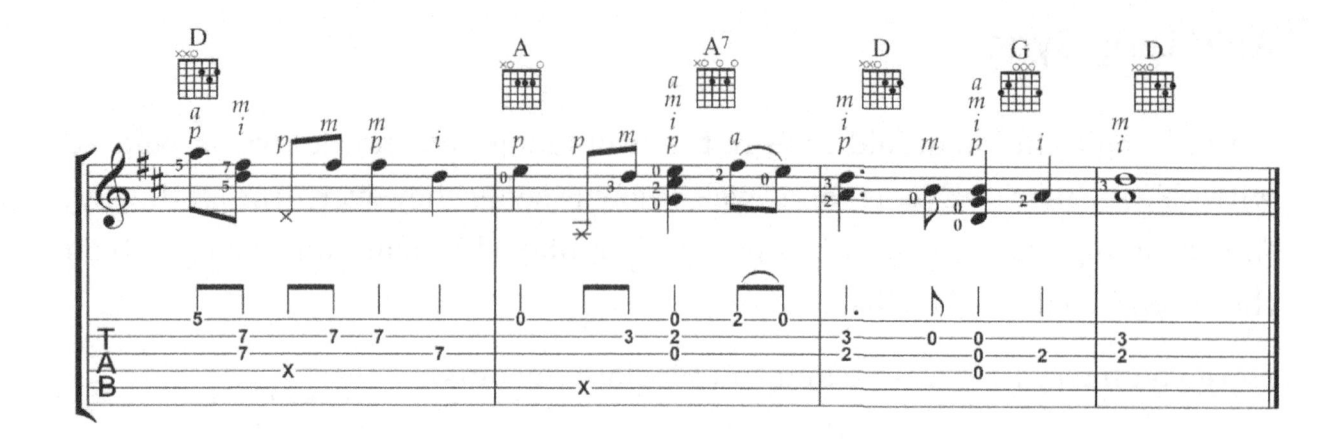

And here's the full version.

Amazing Grace

Originally a Christian hymn from 1779, "Amazing Grace" is immensely popular and has been recorded by hundreds of artists.

The following fingerpicking version is slow, and you can dump the metronome in this one in favor of a rather free tempo, slowing down and accelerating as you see fit, to convey the emotion of this beautiful tune.

As opposed to the two previous songs, this one doesn't have a clear defined bassline, relying instead on arpeggios on top of which we'll add a melody later. Let's check the arpeggios first.

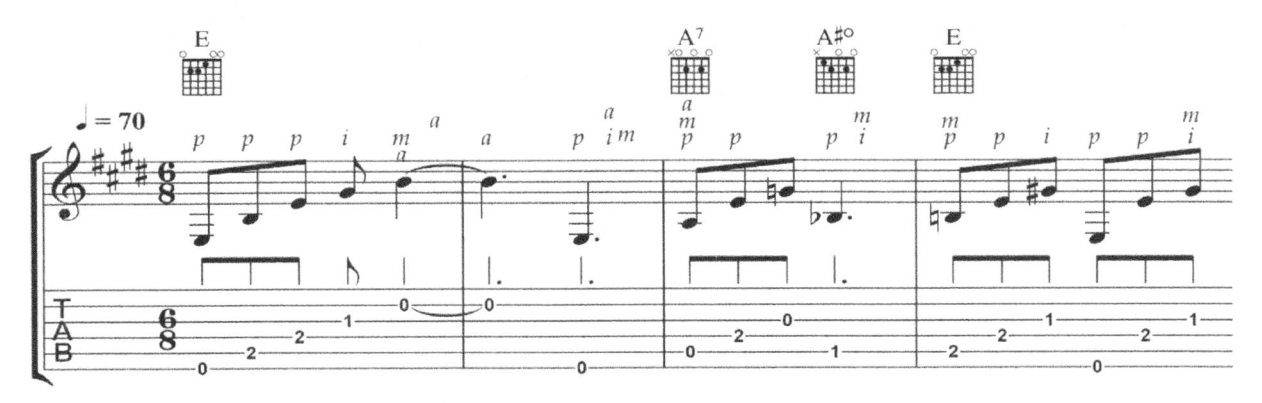

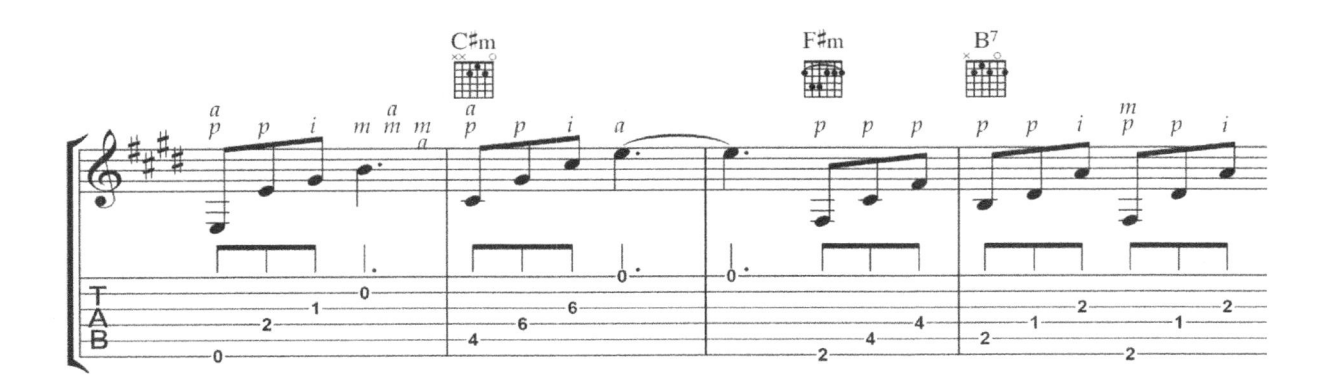

> **Note** : Audio tracks for these melodies are available in the bonus section

Fingerstyle guitar

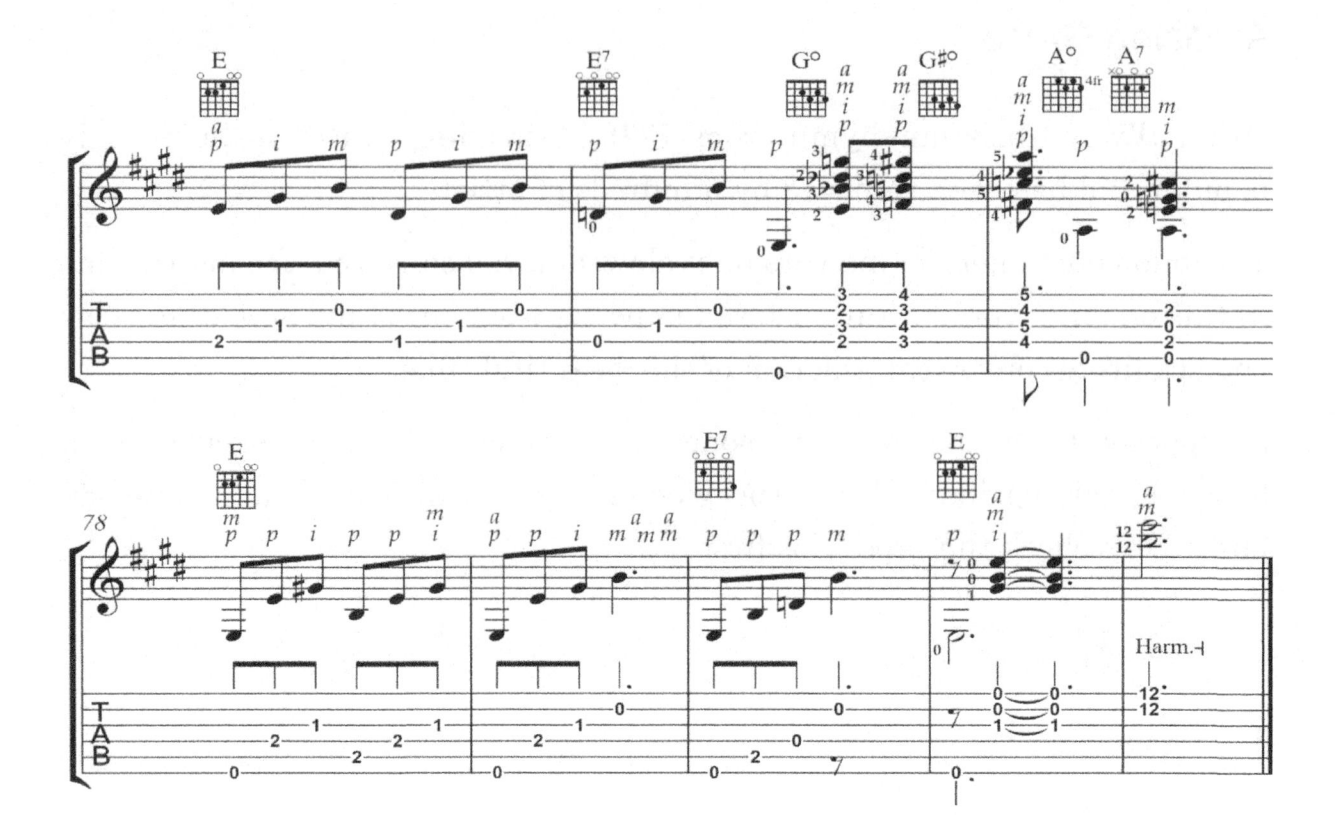

More Pieces

Here's the melody.

Fingerstyle guitar

And now arpeggios and melody together.

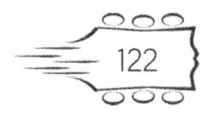

Conclusion

You've made it.

You're at the end of this book but at the beginning of your fingerpicking journey.

With what you've learned through this book, you now have the tools to play fingerpicking guitar songs. Now the only thing that separates you from becoming a truly advanced player is practice. The amount of dedication you put into learning and practicing new songs and skills will dictate how far you will get in this path.

If you want to accompany singers, bands, or your own voice, you're ready for it. With what you've learned here, you're ready to learn most of the songs you'll encounter. You'll still have to put in the time to learn the songs, but now you have the tools to do so.

If, on the other hand, you want to be a jaw-dropping one-man-band virtuoso, you can also do so. It simply takes more practice and time polishing the skills you've learned in this book. In your path you'll probably learn advanced techniques we didn't cover in this book, like combining tapping and percussion, "cascading" harp harmonics, or detuning strings on the fly. These are high-level techniques that wouldn't make sense in a book like this, but that you'll encounter on your path to expertise.

Decide where you want to be and work towards that goal. But don't overthink it too much - you can always iterate later. Perhaps now you're playing in a band and you want to use fingerpicking in a few songs. Then later you might want to start a career as a singer-songwriter and you'll use the same skills to accompany your own voice. And later, you might want to level up those skills and become a Tommy Emmanuel type of instrumental virtuoso.

This is a beautiful journey you're in. It's the journey of mastering an instrument, of taking one of the most common musical tools in existence and using its potential to an extent few do. It means taking something ordinary and making it extraordinary. And it means facing songs and techniques that look intimidating at first, armed with your guitar, a metronome, and patience, and working through them until they become your allies in the artistic pursuit of expressing yourself.

Good luck and enjoy the path!

Farewell

Pssssttttt....

What are you doing here? Are you lost?

Do people even look at the last pages of a book?

Jokes aside, I hope you enjoyed this book. I certainly loved the process of writing it.

If you enjoyed this book, could you take 2 minutes to leave a review about it?

Reviews are the lifeblood for small publishers and help us get our books into the hands of more guitarists like you.

We read every review personally and appreciate each one of it.

To leave a review, simply go to the platform you purchased the book from and type in your review.

With that said, here's Guitar Head signing off!

Until next time then? I'll see you in another book.

THE END

Made in United States
North Haven, CT
19 June 2025